" The Object Lessons series achieves something very close to magic: the books take ordinary—even banal—objects and animate them with a rich history of invention, political struggle, science, and popular mythology. Filled with fascinating details and conveyed in sharp, accessible prose, the books make the everyday world come to life. Be warned: once you've read a few of these, you'll start walking around your house, picking up random objects, and musing aloud: 'I wonder what the story is behind this thing?'"

Steven Johnson, author of *Where Good Ideas Come From* and *How We Got to Now*

" Object Lessons describes themselves as 'short, beautiful books,' and to that, I'll say, amen. . . . If you read enough Object Lessons books, you'll fill your head with plenty of trivia to amaze and annoy your friends and loved ones— caution recommended on pontificating on the objects surrounding you. More importantly, though . . . they inspire us to take a second look at parts of the everyday that we've taken for granted. These are not so much lessons about the objects themselves, but opportunities for self-reflection and storytelling. They remind us that we are surrounded by a wondrous world, as long as we care to look."

John Warner, *The Chicago Tribune*

"In 1957 the French critic and semiotician Roland Barthes published *Mythologies*, a groundbreaking series of essays in which he analysed the popular culture of his day, from laundry detergent to the face of Greta Garbo, professional wrestling to the Citroën DS. This series of short books, Object Lessons, continues the tradition."

Melissa Harrison, *Financial Times*

"Though short, at roughly 25,000 words apiece, these books are anything but slight."

Marina Benjamin, *New Statesman*

"The Object Lessons project, edited by game theory legend Ian Bogost and cultural studies academic Christopher Schaberg, commissions short essays and small, beautiful books about everyday objects from shipping containers to toast. *The Atlantic* hosts a collection of 'mini object-lessons'. . . . More substantive is Bloomsbury's collection of small, gorgeously designed books that delve into their subjects in much more depth."

Cory Doctorow, *Boing Boing*

OBJECT LESSONS

A book series about the hidden lives of ordinary things.

Series Editors:

Ian Bogost and Christopher Schaberg

Advisory Board:

Sara Ahmed, Jane Bennett, Jeffrey Jerome Cohen,
Johanna Drucker, Raiford Guins, Graham Harman,
renée hoogland, Pam Houston, Eileen Joy, Douglas
Kahn, Daniel Miller, Esther Milne, Timothy Morton,
Kathleen Stewart, Nigel Thrift, Rob Walker, Michele White.

In association with

LOYOLA
UNIVERSITY
NEW ORLEANS

Georgia | Center for
Tech | Media Studies

BOOKS IN THE SERIES

sock

KIM ADRIAN

Bloomsbury Academic
An imprint of Bloomsbury Publishing Inc

B L O O M S B U R Y
NEW YORK · LONDON · OXFORD · NEW DELHI · SYDNEY

Bloomsbury Academic

An imprint of Bloomsbury Publishing Inc

1385 Broadway   50 Bedford Square
New York   London
NY 10018   WC1B 3DP
USA   UK

www.bloomsbury.com

BLOOMSBURY and the Diana logo are trademarks of Bloomsbury Publishing Plc

First published 2017

© Kim Adrian, 2017

Library of Congress Cataloging-in-Publication Data
A catalog record for this book is available from the Library of Congress.

ISBN: PB: 978-1-5013-1506-0
      ePub: 978-1-5013-1507-7
      ePDF: 978-1-5013-1508-4

Series: Object Lessons

Cover design: Alice Marwick

Typeset by Deanta Global Publishing Services, Chennai, India
Printed and bound in the United States of America

For James

"*I wanted to run after him, but remembered that it is ridiculous to run after one's wife's lover in one's socks; and I did not wish to be ridiculous but terrible.*"

LEO TOLSTOY, *THE KREUTZER SONATA*

CONTENTS

INTRODUCTION

When I tell people I'm writing a book about socks I generally get one of two reactions. The first is frankly dumbfounded. Questions arise, such as, "Why?" or, "What can you possibly say about socks?" or, "Is it a children's book?" The second reaction is closer to delight. Socks! The people in this camp often find immediate humor in the idea of a book on this subject, though I'm not sure why, because even if I much prefer this response to the first, the truth is, I personally don't find socks funny. Mildly amusing, yes, in limited contexts, but not ha-ha just because they're socks. No, I take socks seriously, otherwise why would I be writing a book about them? Well, maybe because I said I would. Actually, that's pretty much it in a nutshell. But in order to write a book about socks, I've had to take them seriously, especially since I'm not a sock expert to begin with. As a matter of fact, there aren't that many sock experts to speak of. Sure, there are a few industry leaders who know the complicated, but not too complicated, ins-and-outs of sock production, and a handful of fashion designers who take a somewhat highbrow interest in the humble sock, and an art historian in

Canada who once put together a museum exhibit on socks, and, of course, there's Milton N. Grass—the lone serious historian of the sock, at least in English (which isn't to say there are other sock historians working in other languages; there aren't, as far as I'm aware), and certainly there's the lady at my local yarn store—who tried, unsuccessfully, I'm afraid, to teach me how to knit socks—and she definitely knows a thing or two about them, but in terms of the deeper ontological mysteries hidden in that object we call a sock, there's, like, no one.

Even Grass's *History of Hosiery*, though an admirable tome and essential reading, clearly, for someone in my position, is peculiarly limited, as Grass's views on the origins of the sock are unapologetically creationist. For example, concerning the beginnings of footwear in general, he wrote (in 1956), "The heat of the desert sands may have inconvenienced our early ancestors . . . after they had left the Garden of Eden." This inconvenience, claims Grass, led to the invention of sandals. At another point, on the matter of when and why people started wearing clothes in the first place, he writes:

Man was born naked! Being born naked he had all the clothing that Nature ever intended him to have. Certain fishes are covered with scales, birds have feathers and some animals have heavy wool or hair covering their bodies. In this respect early man did not differ from other animals. A coat of coarse hair covered his body from head to foot.

Grass justifies this assertion on the basis of a Biblical insight: "The elder son of Isaac and Rebecca is called 'Esau', and the name Esau means, literally, 'covered with hair.'" He goes on to say that we only became hairless when the sun and air of the tropical regions ("where," he notes, with confounding circularity, "man most probably originated") caused our head-to-foot coat to disappear. But Grass wasn't technically a scholar; he wrote *History of Hosiery* as an enthusiastic industry man with an ardent interest in his product. Years later, proving that true passion knows no bounds, he penned, with his wife, Anna, a detailed biography of William Lee, the inventor of the stocking frame.

I should mention here, as well, Jeremy Farrell, whose contribution to the field, *Socks and Stockings*, is an interesting read, to be sure, although not nearly as far-reaching as Grass's book. In addition, there are a few technical, production-oriented pamphlets, dozens—if not hundreds—of knitting books specializing in sock patterns, a handful of surprisingly sock-attentive blogs, a pretty shocking number of sock-centered Twitter feeds, and, within the larger literatures of fashion and textile history, every now and again, the occasional mention of socks. So, I'm not completely alone here in sockland, but I am lonely, which is a bit odd if you think about it, considering how commonplace the object in question is.

Normally, I write about personal things—personal essays, memoir, that sort of thing—and at first, I thought that writing about socks wouldn't be so different, because socks *are* personal—they are intimate and essentially domestic. And domesticity has always been, for me, a fixation. I was going to say a kind of "faith," but I don't want to romanticize things. In any case, I am, at heart, a woman who loves teacups and potted plants and fresh-baked bread and children's toys scattered on the floor and laundry on the line and the smell of onions cooking slowly in oil on the stove. For years—all of my adult life—I have looked to my own home for a sense of security and a source of ordinary beauty, which is my favorite kind. In writing about socks, I thought I'd be writing about something beautiful in an ordinary way, something small and humble and soft and intimate—all adjectives I favor, if not so much on the page, then in real life. But as I researched this book—as I spent more and more time reading about socks, thinking about socks, looking at socks, trying to knit socks, and conducting inventive Google image searches involving the word "socks"—I came to realize that there is no true divide between the home and the larger world, no matter how often we hear things parsed in that way. Because what's small and intimate derives, ultimately, from what's large and impersonal.

This has always been the case on a cosmic scale, of course—we are, literally, star dust (though Milton Grass would have disagreed). But it is true as well even on the more limited scale of human activity. Because while there may have been, at some points in the past, in certain places and periods of time, contexts in which the home existed as a bona fide sanctuary from the larger world, today this is not the case. Today the world exists inside our homes and our homes exist within the larger world as never before—and not simply as digital projections on YouTube, Instagram, Facebook, and Snapchat, but as expressions of our unimaginably intricate global economy, with its incalculable social interdependencies and all too often blood-letting profit margins, all of which are bound up in every toaster, every cell phone, every mattress, every large-screen TV, every baby bottle, every air conditioner, and, yes, every single sock.

This two-way flow between the home and the larger world might not trouble some people, but for committed introverts, such as myself, it presents a deeply problematic situation. Because if I turn inward, toward the home, for a sense of security, balance, beauty, and truth, it is because the larger world—not to put too fine a point on it—terrifies me. I don't think this is because I'm a fearful person. I think it is because I'm a realist. Put it this way: I know crazy when I see crazy—I was raised with crazy—and the world out there, our human intrusions on it, in any case, is nuts. Even when it comes to socks, I assure you, we are acting like lunatics.

FIGURE 1 On the left: Otzi's hay sock. On the right: the corded netting that enclosed it. © South Tyrol Museum of Archaeology/Harald Wisthaler. Courtesy of South Tyrol Museum of Archaeology.

1 SOCKS AND EVOLUTION

Our species descended, of course, not from the hirsute Esau (who already was a human), but from primates covered, like all primates except us, in a thick coat of hair, or, rather, a coat of thick hair. Why our individual hairs thinned to the degree they did, leaving us effectively coat-less, is a mystery no one has answered definitively, although there are many hypotheses ranging from neoteny (the genetic retention of infantile characteristics), to a preemptive method of repelling skin parasites (fleas, at least, do not generally affect us precisely because our body hair is so fine), to the avoidance of those diseases and infections that might otherwise thrive in the bloody, crappy mess at either end of our omnivorous digestive tracks, to the notion that a mysterious—and completely undocumented—aquatic phase of our evolution stripped us of our coat in order to render us more streamlined in the water.

But the most convincing theory I'm aware of is the one that concerns the regulation of body temperature. In his classic on human origins, *The Naked Ape*, Desmond Morris summarizes this theory more or less along these lines: when we stood up on two legs, when we finally became truly bipedal, when our eyes sharpened and, along with them, our minds, when our hands became what they are today—sensitive, highly articulate instruments capable of fine motor coordination and opposable grasping, when we began, with those hands, to make tools, including weapons, and when we became socially complex enough to organize ourselves into cooperative packs, when all of these things combined to create the animal we now know ourselves to be, in short, a first-class predator, we departed from the diet we'd grown up with, evolutionarily speaking—leaves, fruits, nuts, insects, and, perhaps, the occasional salamander—and began to eat larger animals, game animals. This change in our diet, claims Morris, had everything to do with the advent of the hunt—a physically challenging ordeal not well-suited to the more common primate body, with its bowed stature, its rocking gait, and its thick coat of heavy hair. Hunting for game requires the body to go through intense fluctuations in temperature: sprinting greatly heats the system, lying in wait quickly cools it. To accommodate this range, we lost our coat while, at the same time, the number of sweat glands we possess increased. Together, these two new characteristics meant both that we didn't overheat during the most intense part of the chase and that we were also able to rapidly cool down afterward through the evaporative process of sweating.

But what about the cold? And what about the night? For insulation at these times, we acquired a thick layer of subcutaneous fat not found in other primates. This fat *is* our coat. We are insulated just beneath the surface of our bodies, not on top of it.[1] It's a perfect system—as elegant as the thermoregulation of a beehive or a bird's egg. Why, then, do we wear clothes?

Of lice and needles

Textiles are perishable, so there's little direct evidence of clothing through the ages, at least as compared to things like tools, jewelry, weapons, cooking implements, architecture, and our own bone structure. For decades, the question of when we first began making and wearing clothes seemed unanswerable. Yet by studying the DNA sequences of various types of lice over millennia, scientists have recently been able to provide a window onto the general timeframe of our first sartorial inclinations. Lice species, it turns out, are many and highly specialized; on humans, they exist in three distinct forms: head lice, pubic lice, and clothing (a.k.a. "body") lice. Each of these cannot survive except in its own niche environment. The evolution of lice associated with our species tells the story of many of our own most significant genetic changes over time. For example, the emergence of head- and pubic-specific lice seems to point directly to the loss of our ancestors' thicker coat of overall body hair, around 3.3 million years ago, while clothing lice (that's to say, lice that feed off the human body but live in, and only in, our clothes), emerged somewhere between 83,000 and 170,000 years ago.[2]

The thing about human beings—as we're so inordinately fond of reminding ourselves—is that we're smart, so smart, we can outwit nature, at least in short sprints. Clothes are a prime example of this. When our ancestors started moving into the colder climates of Northern Europe, they would have been ill equipped, physiologically speaking, to survive the lower temperatures, and during the last ice age, the homeostasis of the human body was seriously threatened. We would have perished in these contexts if we hadn't figured out how to manipulate our environment and provide our bodies with additional insulation.

Professor John Shea, author of *Stone Tools in the Paleolithic and Neolithic Near East*, has said in a video interview for History.com, that the currency of an ice age is energy, which makes its conservation essential. What allowed our ice age ancestors to survive? What tool got us through the stressors of that era, energetically speaking? "The needle," says Shea.[3] Bone needles allowed us to sew together the skins of animals in order to create clothing that could augment our bodies' defenses against the inhospitable climate. Were socks part of our original wardrobe? No clothes of any kind have been found from that far back; however, there is some indirect evidence—in the form of gracile (which is to say, spindly) toe bones—that our ancestors may have been wearing shoes as early as 40,000 years ago.[4] And if shoes, perhaps socks as well, for the sock is the shadow of the shoe.

The first sock

In *History of Hosiery*, written decades before the discoveries outlined above, Milton Grass, based on his examination of literary texts and various mythologies, claimed that socks and stockings were the very last articles of clothing to be developed. "Many centuries were to elapse after man had enjoyed the benefits and luxury of 'outer-foot-coverings' before he conceived the idea of 'inner-foot-coverings.'" But just because people weren't writing about socks or telling stories about socks doesn't mean they weren't wearing them. Socks are just like that. They generally go unnoticed. Although it's also true that the foot is a complicated thing, and despite the seeming simplicity of the modern sock, inserting a soft, absorbent, insulating, cushioning, protective layer between foot and shoe would have presented enormous difficulties for our distant ancestors, mostly on account of the foot's mobility and the right angle it forms in relation to the lower leg, as well as the flexibility of the toes and ankle joint, which cannot be compromised without also compromising the gait.

Still, humans found ways to make socks—of a sort. For example, the earliest maybe-it-was-a-sock ever discovered is simply a handful of hay that somebody stuffed into a simple leather shoe about 5,500 years ago and left in a sandstone cave in southern Armenia for archaeologists to discover. The shoe—really more of a slipper—is formed to fit the right foot of someone who would, today, wear a women's size US 7. It is made from a single piece of tanned cowhide and is perforated for lacings at both the instep and the heel. Although it shows some signs of wear on the sole, the shoe is in otherwise perfect condition considering its age. This is due partly to the cool, dry conditions inside the cave, partly to the preservative qualities of the thick layer of sheep dung that covered it for thousands of years, and partly to the hay, which may, in fact, not be a sock at all, but a kind of Neolithic shoe-form put in place to keep the leather from deforming when the shoe was not in use.[5]

That said, the oldest definitely-a-sock ever found is also a bunch of hay, about 500 years younger than the maybe-it-was-a-sock. It belonged to the mummy known as "Otzi the Iceman," who sometimes also goes by "Fritz the Frozen," and who was discovered by a German couple hiking in the Otzal Alps in 1991. Deciding to take an unmarked shortcut for their decent, the middle-aged pair stumbled upon the mummy's neat, brown head, knobby spine, and delicate shoulder blades emerging from the ice and gritty loess of a sheltered gully. Helmut and Erika Simon assumed that the body was that of someone more or less like themselves—a modern-day hiker who'd strayed off the official path, and who'd then perhaps gotten waylaid by a storm, or completely lost, and eventually froze to death. In short, they figured the corpse had been lying there for maybe ten or fifteen years because, although clearly desiccated, it seemed to be fully intact.

The Simons reported their find to a local innkeeper, who, in turn, reported it to authorities in both Italy and Austria (the Otzal mountain range straddles the border between those countries). The following day, Austrian authorities attempted to hack Otzi out of the ice using a pneumatic drill, chewing up some of his clothing and a bit of his left hip in the process. The day after that, two well-known mountaineers, Hans Kammerlander and Reinhold Messner, inspected the body and noticed that the tools and clothing near it seemed to be quite ancient. Two days later, Otzi was finally hacked free of his icy tomb by a team working under the leadership of Rainer Henn, a forensic pathologist from Innsbruck University.

Through radiocarbon dating, Henn and his team established that the mummy was approximately 5,000 years old. This constituted a spectacular find, and not just because of the body itself—the bones, tattoos, and organs of which are full of stories—but also because of the wide array of Copper Age artifacts that surrounded it, tools of a skilled and extremely well-equipped huntsman circa 3,000 BCE. These include: an axe; a dagger; a bow; a quiver; two arrows; a dozen arrow shafts; a net for catching game; a little noose for carrying it; two knobs of fungi that seem likely to have had medicinal properties; and something called a *retoucheur* (a kind of pointed chisel for chipping flint).

Otzi was also in possession of a remarkably sophisticated outfit consisting of a loincloth, leggings, a bearskin cap, a hide coat, and one shoe. This last item was a complex construction made of an outer sheath of deer and bear leather, and an inner net of corded grass—a kind of foot-shaped basket. Inside this net was the first definitely-a-sock ever found: another handful of hay.

A short primer on the human foot

The human foot is an awe-inspiring example of anatomical architecture—"a masterpiece of engineering and a work of art," as Da Vinci put it. Containing 26 bones, 33 joints, and over 100 muscles, tendons, and ligaments, it is functionally segmented in four: the forefoot, the midfoot, the hindfoot, and the subtalar joint. Each of these has many jobs, but in essence, the forefoot propels, the midfoot stabilizes, the hindfoot absorbs shock, and the subtalar joint coordinates the bones of the foot with those of the ankle. We stand not on one, but three arches of greater or lesser strength and beauty depending on the foot: the medial longitudinal arch, the lateral longitudinal arch, and the transverse arch. We are not the only bipedal animals—birds, kangaroos, bears, certain mice, and rabbits all spend time on two feet—but we are the only mammals to regularly sustain a bipedal gate.

In order to do so, our big toes are arranged differently than those of other primates in that they extend straight out in front of us. By contrast, a gorilla's big toe angles off medially, as the thumb does on a hand, an arrangement that allows it to gambol among the branches of trees. But on the ground, it is an awkward, bowlegged walker, while the modern Homo sapiens' gait is so elegant that the duration of the various movements involved (the "swing phase," the "stance phase," and the "double support phase") has been scientifically proven to reflect the golden mean in temporal form.[6] In other words, the way we walk expresses a music of motion as perfect, proportionally speaking, as any Mozart sonata.

We are not just bipedal, but uniquely vertical as well, and the plumb drop of our posture affects everything about us, from the size of our brains, to our mating behaviors—including, even, our post-coital tendency to cuddle and nap, which some speculate serves to postpone the moment the female stands and walks away from the male (as all other female primates do immediately following coitus), since the more or less vertical orientation of the vagina in the standing human quickly drains the canal of seminal fluid, thus lowering the chances of impregnation.

Walking upright on two feet also dictates the unusual relationship of our spine to the weighty, boney masses at either end of it—the head and pelvis. The latter, for example, is shaped, uniquely, more or less like a bowl, small and deep, with a sturdy floor that supports the contents of our abdomen—contents that rest directly on top of it. Our hip structure is significantly more flexible than that of other primates, whose pelvises resemble something closer to a shoehorn than a bowl. Long in back and low in front, theirs is a shallow structure that makes for an altogether stiffer dynamic between the upper and lower halves of the body. This type of structure has the advantage of allowing easy, frequent transitions between more or less upright (bipedal) and more or less horizontal (quadrupedal) locomotion.

Meanwhile, at the other end of the spine, the human head has evolved into a position that's essentially balanced on the spine's topmost vertebra. In all vertebrates, spines connect to heads through holes in the skull. This hole is called the *foramen magnum* (there are many *foramina*, or holes, in the body, but this one is the "great hole"). In quadrupeds, the foramen magnum can be found directly opposite the face, as the spines of four-footed animals extend horizontally, parallel to the ground. But in primates, the foramen magnum is at the base of the skull, and in humans it is located very near the center of the base of the skull. This accounts for one of the most curious adjunct expressions of our bipedalism: the human face, which is more or less flat and unusually small for our size. The reason for this, explains Daniel Lieberman, a professor of biological sciences at Harvard University, is that the center of gravity for the human head falls slightly in front of the foramen magnum, which is to say, slightly in front of our spine; so the reduced the bulk of our face helps to minimize the natural tendency of the head to fall forward, particularly when we're running.[7]

It's not just the vertical orientation of our spines that helps us to be the upright creatures we are, but the shape of them as well. Our primate cousins have spines that describe an asymmetrical C-curve, like a stem slightly weighted by a flower. But our spines are closer to the shape of an S. Ironically, it is the subtle undulations of our spines that allow for the overall straightness of our form; the S-curve acts like a spring, providing shock absorption for the tremendous downward forces of our vertical existence. Because, in the end, we are essentially columnar: our heads sit on top of our spines, our spines on top of our hips, our hips over our legs, and our legs over our ankles, which, in turn, attach to the supportive platforms of our feet at a more or less perfect right angle.

This is hardly an ideal situation. Think about it: how many tables have you seen with two legs? How many chairs or stools? It's a real feat to maintain balance using only two points of contact with the ground, which is why paleoanthropologist John Napier has described the act of walking, as we humans accomplish it, as "a unique activity during which the body, step by step, teeters on the edge of catastrophe." In fact, we only manage to avoid face planting at each step because our entire system works madly in order to maintain our balance. In particular, three involuntary reflexes—the visual, the vestibular, and the proprioceptive—work together in ways that can be said to mimic the "multiple gyroscopes that inform a pilot about the pitch, roll, and yaw of his plane."[8]

But it is our feet that sustain the physical brunt of our bipedal activity. According to M. David Tremaine and Elias M. Awad, authors of *The Foot and Ankle Sourcebook*, "Your feet take an endless beating and log an average of 1,000 miles each year. As shock absorbers, they cushion millions of pounds of pressure during one hour of strenuous exercise. For example, during a one-mile run, your feet carry a total weight of up to five tons."[9] An average person takes almost nine thousand steps a day,[10] while over the course of an average lifetime, each foot will "flex, stretch and contract some 300 million times, yet remain functionally intact."[11] But what may be most remarkable of all is the fact that our feet do these things with minimal equipment, just a little extra fat for cushioning, some thicker skin for protection, a few nails. . . . And even then, the fat and skin, when all is said and done, provide barely a half-inch buffer zone between the mechanical bone-and-muscle structures of our feet and the ground. It's not much, especially when you consider that, over the decades, the fat pads thin and the skin dries and cracks. Shoes help, but they also hurt. Indeed, it's usually because of the constraints of our shoes that our feet grow bunions, our arches fall, and our toes become gracile and misaligned. As the authors of *The Foot and Ankle Sourcebook* put it: "If your feet could 'think', they would probably scheme to revolt."[12]

Sock-as-foot-dressing

This is where socks come in. With them, we give our feet a little extra protection, a bit love. Some coziness. They offer not only warmth and cushioning, but also a kind of pedic embrace. Shaped like a foot, the parts of a sock are named after it: toe, heel, ankle, and instep. But this wasn't always the case. When socks were made of hay, they had no parts to speak of and were likely just called "hay," in whatever language our Neolithic ancestors spoke.

The first recorded mention of socks—or, at least, "inner foot coverings," to use the term favored by Milton Grass—dates from the eighth century BCE, when the Greek poet Hesiod wrote in his poem *Works and Days* (a kind of lyrical advice column), "Around your feet, tie your sandals made from brutally hunted oxen skin and, under these, dress them in *Piloi*."[13]

We don't know what *piloi* looked like, but we do know that the word is the plural of the Greek *pilos*, meaning "felt," so it seems reasonable to imagine some kind of matted wool wrapped around the foot. In other words, *piloi* probably didn't have parts—like "ankles" and "insteps"—but instead were closer to the hay socks Otzi wore, in the sense that they were something one applied to one's foot: a kind of dressing. Moss, leaves, grass, matted animal fur, tufts of cotton or other soft vegetable fibers would also have made likely candidates for this sort of thing. These earliest of socks would have depended entirely upon the outer foot covering—the shoe, slipper, or sandal—for their shape and structure. For example, the felted *piloi* Hesiod describes seem to have been kept in place by sandal lacings. In a similar fashion, Otzi's hay socks were held together by grass nets, which were, in turn, protected by leather uppers. And if the person in possession of the women's size US 7 foot back in Neolithic Armenia actually did use the hay as a sock and not simply as a shoe-form, the leather slipper would have functioned as much as a sock-container as it did a foot-container.

I imagine the process of dressing the foot with hay or other natural materials would have been pretty similar to the way I used to place small tufts of wool around my toes before sliding my feet into *pointe* shoes when I danced ballet as a girl. The first step in this optimistic but ultimately futile ritual was to tease apart the wool—fluff it up. I would then carefully mold it around my toes before gingerly slipping the whole configuration into the cruel but beautiful slipper with its "toe box" and satin ribbons. The wool helped to alleviate the pain that naturally accompanies spinning and jumping on one's toes, but only for a while, because it would inevitably shift as I danced, clumping up in some places, thinning out in others, and eventually matting to such a degree that any benefit became negligible. In general, I suppose the sock-as-foot-dressing would have presented exactly these same kinds of drawbacks for our ancestors. Still, soft material arranged around the foot would have been our best option, at least until the advent of weaving.

Necessity of socks

Coziness, of course, is not the primary function of a sock. Socks provide very real protection for our feet. For example, they prevent chafing against our shoes, which is a more serious concern than you might think, as blisters can be deadly. This was famously illustrated by the unfortunate death of Calvin Coolidge Jr., who neglected to wear socks one day while playing tennis on the White House grounds. The sixteen-year old got a blister on the middle toe of his right foot. It became infected and, as this was before the advent of penicillin, the infection soon spread to his blood. The boy died of sepsis within a week.

Socks also absorb a rather astonishing amount of sweat. One pair of feet possesses more than 250,000 sweat glands (no, it's not a typo). These glands pump out about one "egg cup's worth" of sweat per day.[14] Curiously, our foot-sweat, in its natural state, is not particularly smelly. This is because our bodies produce two different types of sweat—eccrine, which is composed almost entirely of salt and water, and apocrine, which is thicker, a little milky, and associated with body odor. The sweat glands in our feet are of the eccrine type, so while they may make things moist, they don't make things smell. It's actually our shoes that make our feet stink. Or rather, to be a little more precise, it's the bacteria that feed on the dead skin shed by our feet that smells so bad. Or rather, again, it's the excretions of this bacteria—excretions that ferment in the eccrine bath pumped out by the quarter-million sweat glands I just mentioned; and as shoes prevent the natural evaporation of that sweat, when we wear them, everything just kind of stews together to create that particular skank we associate with feet. In any case, socks are clearly of some help in this regard, since they both absorb sweat and are easily washed between wearings. Socks also help prevent fungal infections, which thrive in moist conditions.

But perhaps the most important health function of socks is the role they play in the prevention of two very serious conditions: frostbite and trench foot, both of which are caused by prolonged vasoconstriction in the feet. In frostbite, the vasoconstriction occurs for the usual reasons; our bodies get cold and our systems prioritize the flow of blood to our vital organs, leaving our extremities vulnerable to freezing. With trench foot (also called "immersion foot") the etiology is less clear, but for some reason, prolonged exposure to cool, damp conditions also causes the blood vessels in the feet to constrict. When blood doesn't circulate, tissues are starved, and flesh necrotizes. In extreme cases of both frostbite and trench foot, flesh and bone can become gangrenous and may actually fall off. Both of these disorders are common wartime afflictions, and warm, dry, insulating socks are essential for their prevention. This is why, during the First World War (when it's estimated over 20,000 men were afflicted by trench foot), the Red Cross put out their famous call for sock knitters. "Do your bit," read their slogan, "knit SOX."

Woven foot wrappings

Recent evidence indicates that there seems to have been some weaving activity as far back as 27,000 years ago,[15] although it is generally thought that the widespread practice of weaving developed much later than that—in the beginning stages of the agricultural age, around 10,000 BCE. It was only then, when larger human settlements were established, that people began growing fiber crops, such as cotton and flax, and herding sheep. Larger settlements also allowed for more elaborate social cooperation and greater specialization of labor.

In woven fabric, threads are arranged at right angles to one another. The relationship of warp to weft makes for a strong textile, but one with little give, at least when cut on the grain. However, when woven fabric is slanted, either by cutting it on the bias or by simply placing it diagonally in relation to the body, it has much more flexibility.

The first woven socks we know of, called *faciae* in Latin, have been described as "a bandaging or wrapping around the leg"[16]; these were probably thin bands of fabric spiraled around the lower leg and, perhaps, the foot as well. To spiral the fabric places it on the bias, thus increasing its elasticity. *Faciae* would be similar to what are called "puttees" today, which are still sometimes worn in military contexts: tightly bound spirals of twill fabric (or, in some cases, leather) wrapped around the calves. Puttees, it seems, have their pros and cons. According to the website oryansroughnecks.com, a history buff's collection of Second World War facts and ephemera, "In a uniform replete with uncomfortable features (tight, standup collar and breeches) no feature of the uniform is more uncomfortable than puttees. It is also one of the most distinguishing features of the Doughboy uniform and when done correctly nothing looks sharper."

Another method of using woven fabric to cover the foot is the infamous "foot wrap." Exactly what it sounds like, the foot wrap (or *portyanki*) was standard issue for the Russian military until 2013. A foot wrap, sometimes also called a foot cloth, is made with a rectangular piece of fabric, about the size of a large dishcloth, on which the foot is placed at a forty-five-degree angle in relation to the grain of the weave. The wrapping process is a sort of origami-like swaddling, during which the fabric is spiraled, flipped, and twisted around the foot, ankle, and the awkward protuberance of the heel. Foot wraps do not look particularly comfortable to wear, although some soldiers claim they are better than normal socks when properly executed. Like the more ancient foot dressings, foot wraps are only secure once they are inside a boot or shoe. Archaic though it may be, the art of wrapping the foot in fabric strikes me as a good one to know in case of emergency—camping fiascos, for instance, or worldwide Armageddon.

Fitted and knitted socks

A more sophisticated way of making a sock from woven fabric involves cutting and sewing: tailoring, in other words. The tailored sock reflects a fascinating bifurcation in the development of clothing in general. Milton Grass describes this as the difference between clothes that are wrapped around the human form and those that are *put on* individual body parts. The first category—clothes that are wrapped or draped—is generally associated with the cultures of antiquity as well as contemporary cultures with still vital roots in the deep past, particularly in parts of Asia, Africa, and the dwindling aboriginal tribes of South America. This type of clothing includes cloaks, togas, and loin clothes—whole-cloth creations, complete pieces of fabric that essentially hang from the body. Tailored clothes are those that closely fit individual body parts, and they are a much more recent development, of which the Roman *udone* may be one of the very first examples. An *udone* was made of four or five pieces of fabric sewn together to create a kind of anklet, similar to the Japanese *tabi*, which is still worn today (though mostly, I think, for nostalgic purposes).

Tailored socks and their sartorial descendants, woven stockings, were an enormous improvement over dressed and spiraled or twisted socks, yet, being woven, they remained somewhat inflexible and, I imagine, a bit baggy, even when cut on the bias, making all these options less than ideal when it comes to covering the foot. No, the perfect sock was hardly possible until the advent of knitting.

Nålbinding seems to have been the prototype of the craft we know today as knitting, although it is different in some significant respects. For example, nålbound fabric is created with a single needle and many short lengths of yarn spliced together, whereas knitting uses anywhere between two and five needles and one continuous (or, at least, theoretically continuous) strand of yarn. The structure of nålbinding is also different and, generally speaking, less flexible than that of knitting. Still, as Richard Rutt, the author of *A History of Hand Knitting*, puts it, "To say that knitting developed from nålbinding . . . is conjectural, but reasonable."

—

If you google the words "world's first sock," the most popular image to surface will probably be that of a very long, very narrow, faded tomato-red object, foot-shaped with a separate compartment for the big toe, and a heel cup. This sock was made by nålbinding and was discovered in Egypt in the nineteenth century. It dates from about 300 to 500 CE. It's hard to imagine a foot that this sock would actually fit, but apparently there was somebody living in ancient Egypt with a wicked long, wicked narrow foot who liked to wear socks with their sandals. Interestingly, the first evidence of true knitting also comes to us in the form of a sock, or rather, three socks. These are dramatic, two-color cotton creations of quite elegant construction, often called "the Coptic socks" because they, too, were found in Egypt, with the oldest of the three dating from between 1000 and 1200 CE, and the others from around 1100 to 1300 CE.

Knitting socks, I know from bitter experience, is not as straightforward a task as it may at first seem because socks are not really, as they appear to be, simply little bags for our feet, and sock knitting requires careful math, or, at least, the ability to mentally project a three-dimensional, foot-like form (complete with heel and toe, as well as a pretty dramatic angle for the foot-to-leg-join) onto a seemingly unrelated geometry of angles and flaps. What I mean is, you have to knit squares where it really doesn't seem logical to knit squares, and triangles where it seems sort of logical, but only if you don't think too hard; and to do both of these things you need to add and subtract stitches in sequences that seem in direct contradiction to common sense. But in the end, it all works out. At least, so I've been told. I have knit literally dozens of sweaters, some of them quite complex with cables and color changes. I've knit hats and pillows and purses and really, really long scarves with multiple textures, but socks remain beyond me. Socks are fussy and, of course, there are always two of them, which, in my view, is one too many. All of which I point out to highlight the fact that the Coptic socks are not only splendid examples of two-color knitting, but *socks* as well, which would seem to indicate that the craft of knitting had probably been around for quite some time at the point of their creation—decades, at least, more likely centuries.

Old as it is, knitting is not nearly as ancient as weaving. As Milton Grass and others have pointed out, there are no myths about knitting, as there are about weaving; there are no gods or goddesses associated with it; and there's no evidence of the craft of knitting to be found in ancient art and artifacts. But, boy, I bet those Egyptians were stoked when knitting finally hit the scene. Because the fact of the matter is, only the sock made by knitting—true knitting, not nålbinding—can accommodate the wiggling, pounding, twisting, leveraging, springing, and bending of the human foot with no restriction to speak of. Indeed, knitting is so perfectly suited to the production of socks that the two most commonly knit fabrics go by names intimately related to the production of hosiery: stockinet (or stockingnette, or "stocking-net") and garter. Stockinet is what most people picture when they think of knitting: interlocking v's on one side and nubby, horizontal bars on the reverse. The stockinet stitch creates a very smooth, elastic fabric, but it tends to roll at the edges. Garter stitch results in pronounced horizontal ridges that lie absolutely flat, and for this reason it is often used in edge treatments on stockinet fabrics. In all likelihood, garter stitch got its name from the fact that it was frequently knit at the tops of stockings, right where garters would have been attached.

In terms of structure, hand-knit fabric is basically a field of interlocking loops, created one row at a time. Each row is made stitch-by-stitch, or, put another way, loop-by-loop, with every new loop being drawn through the loop directly below it (unless you're doing something fancy—like making lace). Knitting is more portable than weaving since it can be held in the hands or on the lap, and carried in a small purse. It differs from weaving in this important way as well: knitting allows for the creation of complex three-dimensional structures *as* the fabric is being created. In other words, there's no need to cut knitted fabric into pieces, then sew them back together in order to accommodate volume. Common shaping techniques in knitting include changing the number of stitches per row ("increases" and "decreases"), as well the temporary retention, on a spare needle, of a discrete stretch of the work, to be rejoined later in the process. This latter technique is one that allows for many sculptural possibilities, including a kind of rounded cup shape. With tricks such as these, knitted garments are uniquely capable of fitting the curves, angles and bulges of the human body, including even the awkward protuberance of the heel and the right angle of the foot in relation to the lower leg *without the use of a single seam.*

No big deal, you say? Well, when was the last time you went around with a seam in your sock? Even a slightly twisted or holey sock can be exquisitely vexing, annoying to the point of real distraction. But generally speaking, we don't give our socks a second thought—at least until there's something wrong with them. My point is this: before the practice of knitting, there was always something wrong with socks.

Actually, it's all a bit messy

One of the discoveries of contemporary historical science has been to show that historical time cannot be conceived of as linear and unique because history is made up of a number of timescales of different lengths which lie over each other. There are absolutely specific events; there are situations of longer duration called conjunctures; and finally there are structures which last even longer. . . . Clothing is affected by all three of these timescales.

— Roland Barthes, *The Language of Fashion*[17]

The word "sock" comes to us from the Greek word *sykchos*, which originally described a soft, low-cut leather boot, perhaps of Persian origin. *Sykchoi* were worn almost exclusively by women. Men who wore them were either considered effeminate or did so in theatrical settings, where their footwear signified a clown-like character. In Rome, the *sykchos* became a *soccus*, but it remained a soft leather shoe. Even in its first incarnation in Old English, the word *socc* still meant a light slipper.

I'll be frank; I don't have the patience to parse the incredibly complicated history of the sock as it moved up and down the leg, in and out of consciousness, on and off the foot, through the ages. Suffice it to say that over the last several centuries, socks have flitted in and out of focus as a garment in their own right. For example, there were once something called *scanc-beorgs* (shank-guards) and something else called *scinc-hose* (skin hose), both of which may or may not have influenced the development of *soccas* (short socks). Hose (sometimes called *chausses*) were originally nothing but cloth or leather casings for the legs.

Sometimes these were worn with soccas, and sometimes they weren't. Sometimes soccas and hose were sewn together, and sometimes not. Sometimes hose were sewn to *braies* (medieval drawers), and sometimes they weren't. At other times, hose, braies, and soccas were stitched into a single garment, and sometimes long soccas were connected to braies with garters and the hose were omitted. It's all extremely complicated and hard to keep track of. But this seems worth noting: the evolution of the sock that I've been tracing is more or less as that garment developed in Western cultures, yet socks and sock-like articles were also developed in other cultures, along similar though not identical lines. For example, the Anasazi (an aboriginal people from the area we now know as the Four Corners) made a type of footwear referred to by archaeologists as "shoe-socks"—extremely flexible, low boots, or, if you like, extra-sturdy socks. They made these using a knotless netting technique through the holes of which they interwove softer material, including, in at least one instance, human hair. Some of these smart-looking creations date back to between 1100 and 1300 CE, and seem a near perfect marriage of shoe-plus-sock: a Reese's peanut butter cup for the foot, if you will.

This, too, seems a worthy aside: in the Middle Ages, in Europe, men's hose, socks, and drawers became a single clinging garment known as "skin tights." Often sewn in flashy color combinations, these were so form fitting that they "showed every muscle and tendon of the thighs and legs,"[18] for which reason they were considered quite risqué. So, needless to say, all the young men wore them.

The stocking frame

Though knitting seems to have originated around 1000 CE, woven and sewn socks and stockings remained the norm for centuries after that date, at least in Europe, where they persisted into the eighteenth century. Many of the very earliest knitted artifacts have been found in the graves of wealthy individuals. This might mean that knitted garments were something only the rich wore, or it might mean that the garments of the rich simply survived better than those of the poor because their graves were better—more airtight, more secure. In any case, the path these artifacts trace seems to indicate that knitting spread from northern Africa to Spain and from there to the rest of Europe, but rather slowly. At least, there is "no record that the art of hand-knitting was known in England before the beginning of the 15th century."[19] However, by the middle of the sixteenth century, knitted and fulled (or felted) caps were commonly produced in both England and France, yet "references to knit hose . . . are not plentiful"[20] even into the sixteenth century.

The first record of knitted stockings in England occurs in 1560, in reference to a black silk pair given to Queen Elizabeth, who promptly decided that these, being so "pleasant, fine and delicate," would be her new staple, and that she would "weare no more cloth stockings."[21] Fairly soon thereafter, a thriving cottage industry of stocking-knitting grew up in England, and knitted stockings became so popular that "even allowing for exaggeration, up to a quarter of a year's wages could be spent on them."[22]

And then something very funny happens, very suddenly, in the history of the sock and its cousin, the stocking (which at the time were more or less what we refer to as "thigh-highs" now). This story has a number of variants, but my favorite goes like this: A man named William Lee. . .

> married secretly while he was a student at Cambridge. This was against the statutes of the university at the time, and he was expelled. His lovely wife, who had learned the art of hand-knitting, was compelled to support both Lee and their infant child by knitting stockings. In despair at the low estate to which he had fallen, suddenly, while watching his wife knit, he conceived the idea of inventing a machine which would knit, and so free his wife from the necessity of supporting the little family.[23]

In 1589, after much figuring, fussing, dreaming, and drawing, William Lee succeeded in building what he called the stocking frame. This was a mechanized knitting loom—a large boxy construction, operated by two people. It had sinkers, pressers, jacks, and a long series of tiny hooked needles. In one motion, those needles could complete an entire row of knitting, as opposed to the needles held by hand-knitter, which can complete but a single stitch at a time. William Lee figured he was onto something big, and for good reason. His machine was truly ahead of its time, coming almost two hundred years in advance of what's normally considered the start of the Industrial Revolution. Excuse me, but I think this deserves an emoticon.

: O

Unfortunately, Lee never earned the riches he'd so hoped for, because when he applied for a patent from the queen, she denied him—twice—saying that the stockings produced on his loom were shabby things, much too coarse. In fact, there's some speculation that Elizabeth may have been protecting the profitable business of knitting as it existed under her reign—a thriving cottage industry that supported a great number of very old and very young people, invalids, and women who worked from home making a product—no matter how laboriously—that commanded a decent price.

Lee eventually moved to France and tried to make a go of things there, but he had little success, and died a financially ruined man in Paris. To say it's ironic that he never saw any monetary reward for his invention doesn't quite cover the drama of Lee's bad luck, seeing as how his stocking frame is the clear antecedent of even the most sophisticated sock- and stocking-making machines in operation today. Yes, these machines are now digitized. Yes, they are now blindingly fast. Yes, they knit in the round, rather than flat (Lee's socks and stockings were knit in two dimensions and had to be seamed up the back). But the fact remains that, in basic conception, the production machinery of today's hosiery industry can still be traced directly to Lee's stocking frame, a machine that, had it caught on during its inventor's lifetime, may conceivably have kick-started the Industrial Revolution into action roughly two centuries earlier than Watt's steam engine, Hargreaves' spinning jenny, and Whitney's cotton gin did in the second half of the eighteenth century. And who knows what that would have meant, where it might have led? What strange wormhole of alternate reality we might have tumbled down if Elizabeth had granted Lee his patent?

Fast-forward four centuries

Over time, as improvements were slowly added to it, the stocking frame eventually took off. After Lee's death, his brother, James, and a former apprentice named Aston added fixed sinkers to the machine, which allowed the gauge of the final product to be doubled, thus creating a much finer fabric. It also seems likely that this innovation allowed the machine to be operated by one person, rather than two. This second generation of the stocking frame—more effective, more user-friendly—grew in popularity, and the craft of frame knitting spread. In England, at least for a while, the hosiery business was a very good one to be in, particularly when the frames were used to produce luxury silk stockings for the upper classes (the working classes continued to knit their socks by hand, using wool). Further improvements to Lee's invention, including "trucks," "wheels," "sleys," "caster backs," "hanging bits" and "front stops,"[24] all resulted in an even more refined product and an easier-to-use machine.

As the stocking frame spread throughout Europe and into the Americas, a system of countless middlemen grew up, connecting frame owners to frame workers, to yarn suppliers, to consumers. Stockings of all types were now knit on frames, not just the higher-end products. As the Industrial Revolution rolled on, technical improvements in production methods changed the entire economic substructure of stocking frame knitting. And when steam-powered spinning machines lowered the cost of yarn, stockings began to be produced very cheaply—so cheaply that they became grossly overproduced, and as a result the men (for they were always men) operating the frames were so poorly compensated that they found it "almost impossible to keep body and soul together."[25] This situation led to the famous Luddite Rebellion, spearheaded by a stocking frame operator with a bit of a bad-boy reputation named Ned Ludd. Ludd started things off on March 11, 1811, by smashing two stocking frames in Nottingham. Sixty-three additional frames were broken that same night, and two hundred more were destroyed over the next three weeks throughout Northwest England. Needless to say, Industrialism rolled on, and the stocking frame itself continued its mechanical evolution, first with the addition of steam power, then with a circular, rather than a two-dimensional, arrangement of its needles, which allowed socks and stockings to be knit seamlessly, in the round.

Further refinements to the production of socks include the 1938 invention of the nylon monofilament, the establishment of assembly line factories, and, most recently, computer-aided design, which allows for extremely complex visual decorations—whole scenes, elaborate puns—to be knit directly into the body of a sock. Computer-aided design also means that a single sock may now contain dozens of variations in terms of thread-thickness and knitting gauge, so that each part of the foot can potentially be embraced by a slightly different kind of fabric. The end result of such elaborate attention to detail is what's known as a "high functioning" sock, equipped with features like "stay up technology," "blister tabs," and "performance footbeds." Today, you even can buy socks outfitted with RFID (radio frequency identification) chips, so that you can more easily pair your socks after the wash. Okeydokey. There are, as well, socks that, when walked in, force "a bladder's worth . . . of urine to circulate through integrated tubes toward microbial fuel cells (MFCs), which contain bacteria that guzzle nutrients and create electricity."[26] In this way, you can charge your cellphone. There are socks made with a rechargeable system of TCE (transcutaneous electrical) nerve stimulation that provide your feet with up to fifteen hours of low-frequency electrical impulses.[27] There are socks that soften your feet with infusions of various emollients slowly released via a gel liner. There are medical socks that compress your feet in a special way if you're a diabetic, and medical socks that compress your feet in a different way if you have varicose veins, and medical socks that compress your feet in a yet another interesting way if you have arthritis. And Hammacher Schlemmer sells "the only cordless plantar fasciitis pain relieving sock" on the market. It's battery operated.

81 billion socks

> I cannot believe that our factory system is the best mode by which men may get clothing. . . . As far as I have heard or observed, the principal object is, not that mankind may be well and honestly clad, but, unquestionably, that the corporations may be enriched.
>
> —Henry David Thoreau, *Walden*

Today, there are many, many socks in the world. Many, many more, certainly, than in Otzi's day, when socks were made of hay and the world population is estimated to have been around 30 million. It's impossible to say exactly how many socks are floating around our planet, but consider this: the Datang Province of China (also known as "Sock City") produces 13.5 billion pairs of socks per year[28]—or slightly less than two pairs per person on the planet. Even so, 13.5 billion pairs of socks accounts for only about one-third of worldwide annual sock production,[29] which puts the total number of new pairs of socks made each year around 40.5 billion, or 81 billion individual socks. But that sounds like mumbly-nada. Like fuzz. How can we truly comprehend such an outlandish number? How to picture it?

81,000,000,000 socks this year.
81,000,000,000 socks next year.
81,000,000,000 socks the year after that.
81,000,000,000 the year after the year after that. . .
And so on.
And so on.
And so on.
Until—?

Generally speaking, we humans have ten fingers and ten toes, which make counting to twenty pretty easy for most of us—though after that, it's always a bit of an imaginative stretch, at least in my experience. Still, we've all seen one hundred things: one hundred acorns, one hundred cars, one hundred cookies, one hundred bullets. We've all seen a thousand flowers, a thousand beads, a thousand words. If I squint, I can even picture 37,673 people because that's how many fit into the bleachers at Fenway Park and I've been to Fenway Park during a sold-out game (though I didn't enjoy it). But 81 billion is just noise. Just words. Even 7.4

billion—which is the current world population—strikes me as unreal, no matter how hard a fact it may be. Of course, it's the kind of fact that's forever shifting, slightly, in ways we can only guess at, but the general direction is clear, and if you visit the website www.worldometers.info, you can watch the human population grow in "real time," as tidy columns of figures tick unevenly but relentlessly upward. It's a chilling sight. Every second, four new humans are born, but only two die. Two new souls a second means our population is swelling by roughly 172,000 people every day.[30] Put another way: every 175 days, we grow by 30 million—or about the same number of people Otzi shared the earth with, in the late Copper Age.

In order to help visitors to their website begin to picture the staggering number of human beings inhabiting the planet today, The Population Institute offers this handy visualization to get one's mind around what one billion of anything actually means: "If you took crisp, new $1 dollar bills, a stack of 1 billion dollars would soar 63 miles high."[31] I appreciate the simplicity and drama of this image, but I think the math is off because, according to US Bureau of Engraving and Imprinting, a new dollar bill is only 0.0043 inches thick, which means 1 billion dollars would actually stack closer to 5.5 miles—still impressive, but not in a knock-your-socks-off sort of way. An amount of 7.4 billion dollars (a buck for each person on the planet) would raise the pile to a height of about 42 miles, which is getting somewhere, I suppose, but ultimately, the thinness of dollar bills seems to diminish the magnitude of a billion rather than amplify it. However, if we apply this same thought experiment to socks, and assume (conservatively, I think) that thickness of the average sock is about one-fifth of an inch, the total number of new socks made each year would stack (flat: one on top of the other) all the way to the moon, and then some.

FIGURE 2 Egon Schiele, *Stehende Frau in Rot* (*Standing Woman in Red*), 1913. Public domain image courtesy of Wikimedia Commons.

2 SOCKS AND DESIRE

Rétifism, with or without the accent, means shoe fetish. *Podophilia* is love of the foot. Sock fetishists go by the name "sock fetishists," because, I suppose, like all things sock-ish, even the extremists lean toward the mundane. *Mundane* comes from the French word *mondaine*, meaning "of this world." Originally, it signified that a thing was clean, proper, elegant, worldly; but today it means something closer to boring. Earthbound. Pedestrian. *Pedestrian* stems from the Latin word for foot—*ped*. It is cousin to pedal, pedicure, and pedigree. To be pedestrian is to walk, not run, dance, or skip. A pedestrian goes about on foot, of course. The adjective is often used in reference to lackluster writing, as in dull and prosaic. *Prosaic* is related to the word *prose*, which, itself, has roots in the Latin word *provorsus*, a compound built from *pro-* (forward) and *vorsus* (turned), in other words, oriented in forward-facing fashion –as when walking. If your writing is prosaic it progresses in a predictable manner, never wavering, swaggering, or wandering. Per*vorsus* is a closely related compound but it means, instead, to turn against or go backward. It is the root of our word *perversion*. If you are perverted, you go against the current, the grain, the prevailing winds.

Perversions are often, but not always, sexual in nature. In the sexual context, according to Kinsey in his now antiquated but still revelatory reports, any sexual activity not in direct service of procreation can be considered perverse. That, needless to say, covers a lot of sexual activity when it comes to human beings, including all those activities Freud termed fetishistic, the most common of which happens to be podophilia: love of the odd and ordinary human foot. The foot that connects us to this earth and our pedestrian activities upon its surface, the most pedestrian of which is, of course, walking—an extraordinary anatomical feat, completely unique in the animal kingdom, and, according to kinesthesiologists, the most complex of all human motor activities.[1] Indeed, walking is such a truly precarious balancing act, we only manage to avoid falling with every step because of the gracefully interwoven interactions of our vestibular, visual, and proprioceptive senses and their neurological links to our feet, which serve as both platforms and levers, all 52 bones and 66 joints working in fine-tuned coordination to keep the bizarre orientation of our almost perfectly vertical structures more or less upright even as we make our way— with or against the current—in this world.

According to a 2007 study out of the University of Bologna, podophilia and related obsessions—love of both shoes and socks—account for 47 percent of all sexual fetishisms.[2] Some writers, including Dr. William Rossi, author of *The Sex Life of Foot and Shoe*, consider the foot to be such an erotic feature of the human body as to essentially constitute a secondary sexual organ. The voluptuous aspects of the foot are many and complex, stemming from a mix of cultural, physiological, and psychological factors, including, for instance, the fact that our feet possess even more nerve endings than our genitals. And, unlike the genitals, our feet speak with nuanced gestures in a language—designated by Rossi as "podolinguistics"—capable of expressing subtle gradations of pleasure, anger, fear, stress, desire, and shame. Perhaps it is because of the exceptional expressiveness of our feet that, in Western cultures, for many centuries, the female foot and leg were subject to a sartorial modesty so absolute as to constitute a hijab of lower body.

It's difficult, now, to fully appreciate how stringent the conventions against the revealing of female legs and feet were for so many centuries in Western European cultures when, today, in many places, women wear sandals, miniskirts, and microshorts as a matter of course. But consider this: in eighteenth-century Spain, when a woman's feet flashed momentarily into view from under her floor-length skirt as she descended from a carriage, the sight was thought to be so dangerously revealing that special doors were constructed for the sole purpose of maintaining the complete pedic privacy of all females. And in France the act of showing your feet was, for a woman, a gesture of such unsurpassed intimacy as to be equated with the loss of one's virginity.[3]

The sexual aspect of the human foot may be at least partly explained by recent studies, which have revealed that those neural pathways in the brain that control sensation in the genitals lie directly adjacent to those that control sensation in the feet. In some people, these pathways may be crossed, overlapped, or merged, which might (or might not—there's a lot going on when it comes to fetishes) account for podophilia. Freud and Jung both famously declared the foot to be a phallic symbol. Others take a more complex view and find in the foot attributes not only of the male sex, but of the female as well. Both polyphallic (all those toes) and polyyonic (the clefts between), both hard and soft, strong and vulnerable, the foot expresses many of the most common tropes and metaphors associated with gendered sexuality. Even the shoe can be seen, like its resident, as symbolically representing both womb and penis simultaneously.

The liminal sock

But what of the sock? That flaccid little bag? It, too, reflects the rich androgyny of the foot, and something more as well, for the sock is so fraught with inside-outside ambiguity as to be not merely sexually uncertain, but *perfectly* marginal—a liminal object par excellence. Nabokov recognized this when he gave us that opening image of Lolita: "She was Lo, plain Lo, in the morning, standing four feet ten in one sock." Literally straddling the transition between girlhood and womanhood, she stands with one foot in a child's sock and the other planted in a nakedness that manages to both infantilize and sexualize her. Presented in this way, we immediately recognize Lolita as a being in flux, like the protean slush in a butterfly cocoon, a scarily amorphous creature caught between two states, inhabiting neither. That single sock also speaks to another, more universal kind of liminality: the human animal discovered in the act of metamorphosing from its "natural," naked state into a *more fully* human one—which is to say, a social animal, clothed and conditioned. (In the very next sentence, Lo becomes Lola, and wears slacks.)

In our socks, and only our socks, we are at least two or three sartorial maneuvers away from being adequately equipped for social interaction. The result, as someone points out in the following Reddit discussion, is that wearing socks and nothing but socks can make you feel "more naked . . . rather than just naked." The thread below concerns a photograph of a statue by Anthony Frudakis erected near the boardwalk in Atlantic City. It depicts a man and woman, naked, skipping through a couple of delicate bronze waves. This classical looking pair brings to mind Giambologna's 1579 bronze sculpture known as *The Rape of Proserpina* (often called *The Rape of the Sabine Woman*). Yet no one's getting attacked here. These two, although unsmiling, are ostensibly having fun—at least the title engraved on the base of the sculpture is "Summer," which implies that the couple is not only enjoying the ocean at its warmest, but the full bloom of their adult sexuality as well.

Both man and woman have one foot in the surf and one foot flying in the air behind them because they're frolicking. But the man's right arm encircles the woman by her waist, and something about the tension of that line, or maybe it's in his jutting jaw, or else her leaping figure (which is more vertical than his, and seems somehow mutely desperate), makes the whole thing feel, as another Reddit commentator puts it a little later in the discussion, a bit "rape-y." In the photograph in question, an anonymous jokester has added a pair of white athletic socks to the tableau; one sock has been neatly tugged onto the man's raised right foot and the other onto the woman's.

vainglorious11
    Somehow it makes the statues kind of obscene. . .

MoarVespenegas
    I don't know why but socks are very sexy.

this_sort_of_thing
    I've read it a few places and it's also true, you always feel more naked when you're naked but wearing socks. Rather than just naked.

[deleted account]
    cartoon horses also look more naked

FederalX
    Um . . . .what?

Seibuh

It's best we don't explore this.

MonkPreston

I fear we may be too late.

antdude

I want to know more!

[deleted account]

It's weird because it makes me want to fap to it. But then I give a second look and I don't find anything to fap to. But the impulse to fap when I see the socks is still there.

headfelloff

My hole feels vulnerable when I'm just in socks, is that weird?

Bataille, Freud, Tournier

"Human life is erroneously seen as an elevation," wrote Georges Bataille in his essay fragment "The Big Toe." This idea is integral to a large and messy metaphor, elaborated at length, albeit in bits and pieces, throughout Bataille's work. The metaphor involves, among other things, the sun and the moon, the erect penis, the eye, the anus, and vertically oriented vegetable forms, such as flowers and trees.

"Only human beings, tearing themselves away from peaceful animal horizontality . . . have succeeded in appropriating the vegetal erection and in letting themselves be polarized, in a certain sense, by the sky."[4] The polarization Bataille speaks of is, he claims, a direct result of our bipedalism, and it is defined, at one end, by our light-filled heads, "raised to the heavens and heavenly things," and, at the other, by our feet, which are planted "in the mud." (Ovid mentions something similar in Book One of *Metamorphoses*: "All other animals look downward; Man, / Alone, erect, can raise his face toward Heaven.") Bataille declares the big toe to be "the most *human* part of the human body" because its form sets in motion the chain reaction of physiological realities that ultimately enable the vertical (or vegetal) erection. After all, it is only because of the forward-facing alignment of our big toe (rather than the medial swing exhibited by the big toes of all other primates) that we are able to use the foot as lever—a propulsive device—rather than as an organ of grasping; and it is this propulsive action that allows us to be fully bipedal; and it is our bipedality that creates our upright posture; and it is our upright posture that dictates the orientation of every part of our bodies including, needless to say, the male member, erect or not. In short, the talus, according to Bataille's calculations, is the true root of the vegetal erection, even as that erection points away from the earth and the humble, muddy toe that enables its celestial aspirations.

In this same essay fragment, Bataille argues that a sexual fixation on feet betrays a craving for debasement and defilement—a descent into the primordial sludge, a sinking of vital energies from the head to the southern pole of our feet, thus indicating an urge to return to the primitive horizontality of quadrupeds and less developed primates. In a similar vein, Freud described podophilia as being "coprophillic" in nature. Coprophilia is an abnormal interest in feces, and with this adjective, I think Freud meant that the foot fetishist is, above all, interested in olfactory stimulation: a craving for the fetid bouquet we have come to associate with our feet (although, in fact, that distinctive smell is generally present only in feet that have spent time in those tidy bacteria factories we call shoes).

Martin, the narrator of Michel Tournier's story "The Fetishist," has a more generous interpretation of the aromatic aspect of his obsession, an obsession based not on a craving for defilement or scatological thrills, but on an essentially esthetic desire for the perfect distillation of another person's essence. Martin's fixation has mostly to do women's underpants and bras, rather than shoes or socks (although he does throw in the occasional stocking and has a special interest in boots). He explains that his obsession lies precisely at the intersection of women and their "frillies," as he calls them, and he has little to say about women or frillies in isolation from one another, but craves only the peculiar, evanescent emanation that results from the intimate contact of the one with the other. This is why, when his bride shyly strips herself naked on the first night of their honeymoon, he is horrified by the sight of her body, which he considers "sad," "worse than indecent," even "bestial." He finds solace only by burrowing his face into the clothes she has discarded in a pile on a nearby chair. These are still warm and soft and they smell "like new-mown hay in the summer sun." Similarly, Martin has zero interest in underwear that has not yet been worn, because pieces of lingerie merely displayed in shop windows "haven't come alive yet." It is only clothing that has had some contact with a human body that manages, for Tournier's protagonist, the amazing feat of both imbibing *and* expressing "the human soul."

My children's socks

I know exactly what he's talking about. I'm well acquainted with the habit clothes have of absorbing the essence of a person, and expressing that essence in emotionally challenging ways. And no other type of clothing does this more, in my experience, than socks. Specifically, children's socks. More specifically, *my* children's socks.

I'm not a sock fetishist in the usual sense of that term, but I do have a thing about certain smallish foot bags. In fact, my children's socks are—for me—so drenched with the subtle quintessence of their beings that, over the years, I've been forced to develop a pretty elaborate ritual for throwing them away once they've been outgrown. The most important element of this ritual is a cavalier attitude, a feeling of anti-feeling, of unemotionality. This is a rare state for me, one that comes up no more than once or twice a year. At these times, I am a fantastic cleaner because I can throw things away— weed through my family's pack rat existence and streamline our belongings. Baby books, school papers, children's toys and stuffed animals, favorite but badly chipped mugs, long-used but now impossibly misshapen pillows, irritatingly useless tchotchkes from ancient road trips, hand-me-down trinkets from relatives who couldn't bear to throw them away themselves (and so, with cowardice, simply passed them on to us): I am capable, at these rare moments, just once or twice a year, of showing no mercy to things like this, things that do nothing but clutter our small home and stuff my susceptible heart with useless nostalgia. But even in these moods, the most I can do when it comes to my children's socks is make a pile of those that have outlived their usefulness. This pile I then stuff into a paper bag, which I then put in a specially designated corner of my closet, where it awaits the arrival of another, even rarer mood, that of brutal practicality. This state of mind visits me once, maybe, every two or three years and I jump, at those fleeting moments, on the chance to throw out the sock bag. Even then, my ritual dictates that I must kiss many of the more adorable socks, individually, on their way into the trash, which means that by the end of the ordeal, I am no longer quite so brutal or practical, but overflowing with lush maternal grief.

My children's shoes have never had the same effect on me (well, a couple of pairs, maybe, early on), though I have occasionally gotten teary over their pajamas and certain favorite T-shirts or sweaters. But not in the same way I do with socks. This has something to do with their feet, at least their feet before a certain point, because the older my children get, the less their socks strike me as soft and fragile imprints of their souls, and the more I understand that they are, simply, so much dirty laundry. In fact, now that my daughter is a teenager, I can toss her socks in the trash with barely a second thought. But I still have trouble with my son's socks, which is why, as I type this, I can see, tucked among the piles of papers and books on my desk, an unmatched pair of his that, for some inexplicable reason, has wound up here, in my study. One of these is a tiny white tube sock that must have fit him when he was no older than three or four. The other is slightly larger and thinner: a nylon-cotton blend, pale blue. They're both ordinary enough and, of course, serve no purpose floating around my desk—but that's exactly what they've been doing for the last couple of years because, for some reason, I can't bear to throw them away.

In "Notes of a Native Son," James Baldwin describes watching his younger siblings as they looked into the casket of their father, and remarks, "There is something very gallant about children at such moments. It has something to do with their silence and gravity and with the fact that one cannot help them. Their legs, somehow, seem *exposed*, so that it is at once incredible and terribly clear that their legs are all they have to hold them up." Yes, the simple act of standing on two legs can seem absurdly precarious where children are concerned. And if their legs inspire tenderness, their feet, in my experience, inspire an almost painful affection, an affection that bleeds into fear, because, for some reason, the vulnerability of a child seems most concentrated in their feet. That the urge to protect those feet often manifests itself as a kind of swooning in some folks, has—I'm pretty sure—been known for millennia, but the oldest quote I've found dates from 1898, when G. Stanley Hall wrote that the "the interest of some mothers in babies' toes" often expresses itself in "ecstatic and almost incredible" ways.[5]

A little unfinished

> What a frail, easily hurt, rather pathetic thing a human body is, naked; somehow a little unfinished, incomplete.
>
> **D. H. Lawrence**, *Lady Chatterly's Lover*

This is so true—but why? Why should this be the case? Why are we *so* naked when we're naked? Intuitively, it would seem to have something to do with our relatively furless state, but we're not entirely alone in this category. There are a handful of other "naked" mammals: elephants, dolphins, whales, rhinos, armadillos, hippos. But these animals are gray and thick-skinned—there's something armor-y going on. We, on the other hand, are thin of skin, in fact, epidermally hypersensitive (especially in the hands, feet, lips, and genitals), and we come in an oddly earthy range of colors—from blackish-brown to pinkish-white—more reminiscent of mushrooms than metal.

As previously noted, it's generally thought that we lost our heavy coats as a result of the thermoregulation demands bipedality placed on our systems, not so much in a direct cause-and-effect kind of a way, but because the activities bipedalism allowed us to do created a great many more opportunities for overheating than we'd experienced as more anatomically run-of-the-mill primates.

Darwin figured our two-footed gait must have evolved in order to better accommodate our toolmaking abilities. In other words, he believed that bipedalism followed in the wake of the opposable thumb as an adaptation that allowed us to more fully exploit the usefulness of our hands and the expanding array of artifacts we made with them. But since Darwin's time, archaeologists have uncovered a million-year gap between the first evidence of true bipedalism and that of toolmaking, which pretty well puts the kibosh on that theory. So, if it wasn't holding tools that got us going around on two feet, what was it?

Jeremy DeSilva, a professor of anthropology at Dartmouth College, explained to me in a phone interview that bipedalism offers "no obvious locomotor advantage" save one. In fact, walking on two feet comes at the cost of many downsides. For instance, having lost the quadruped's ability to gallop, we became "exceptionally" slow, so slow we can't outpace predators or catch prey. Additionally, two-footed walking has made us relatively clumsy. The only real bonus—and it's a big one—is that getting around on two feet takes significantly less energy than getting around on four.

Once bipedalism got going, according to DeSilva, our ancestors may have exploited an interesting feeding niche on the African savanna about 4 million years ago. Most animals in that environment, at that time, slept during the heat of the day in order to conserve energy, but our ancestors (this theory posits) went out in the sweltering heat of midday to travel from tree to tree, collecting armloads of fruit, precisely because their predators were out of commission, asleep in the shade. This trick not only demanded that their arms be free in order to lug home edibles, but also placed new and much more stringent thermoregulation demands on their physical systems. The loss of our coat seems to have been a direct result of the latter: our body hair thinned to a very fine texture in order to allow us to survive the high temperatures associated with collecting fruit when the sun was at its hottest, while, at the same time, the number sweat glands our bodies contained increased in order to facilitate cooling, and we grew an extra layer of fat to help us stay warm at night.

This is essentially the same chain of interrelated factors archaeologists have cited for decades to explain the loss of our coats within Darwin's bipedalism-as-a-result-of-tool-making framework, only instead of running around, chasing after prey with spears, this more modern theory has it that we lost our coats slogging through the savanna at high noon. In either case, our relative hairlessness would appear to be the result our bipedalism, just as our bipedalism seems to have been the result of our larger brain, or, perhaps, our sharp eyesight, both of which would have allowed us to more carefully scan the savanna for feeding opportunities, particularly when we stood up on our hind legs to do so. But the word "result" in the previous sentence is misleading, because evolutionary changes connect to one another in kaleidoscopically intricate relationships; every physiological aspect of a biological entity works in concert with every other physiological aspect of that entity, even as the entity as a whole exists within and interacts with its larger environmental context. And all of these elements— the whole shebang—shift over grand time scales in patterns of mysterious synchronicity.

But when the last ice age descended, there wasn't enough time for the slow-motion kaleidoscopic permutations of evolution to return to us our heavy coat. This meant there was only one way we could survive in those conditions, and that was with the help of clothes. Without the protection provided by the animal skins early *Homo sapiens* stitched together using bone needles, our species would have perished. So in the end, D. H. Lawrence was right: we really are a little "unfinished," a little "incomplete," at least in certain climatic contexts.

Decoration's deep roots

Necessity. Modesty. Decoration. These are the three reasons usually cited to explain why we wear clothes. On its face, necessity, being an entirely practical consideration, would seem to be the root cause for clothing the body, for the reasons outlined above. The second factor—modesty—is, of course, a social concern; one that manifests in wildly varied forms from culture to culture. The third—decoration—might strike you, as it did me when I first heard it, as a bit frivolous, hardly a causal factor in any case. But J. C. Flügel, in his seminal 1930 work *The Psychology of Clothes*, makes a very convincing case that decoration may in fact be the most important and elemental of the three.

Flügel was Freudian psychiatrist and while his book is full of fascinating insights, the idea he spends the most time exploring is a classically Freudian conundrum: between modesty and decoration there exists a neurotic tension, a tension Flügel considers intrinsically irreconcilable. Modesty motivates us to cover specific parts of our bodies, but the very act of covering a body part necessarily calls attention to it; likewise, every time we indulge in the urge to adorn and accentuate some aspect of our bodies with a decorative gesture, we simultaneously cover or hide that aspect. The two impulses, in short, are constantly cancelling out one another (nowhere is this more obvious than with the bathing suit). This never-ending contradiction of impulses means that all of our clothing ultimately functions as what Flügel termed a "perpetual blush" upon the human form. This is some elegant reasoning, but in the end it's undermined by Flügel's argument regarding the primal roots of the decorative impulse, an argument so convincing that modesty comes to seem a mere afterthought—in the grand scheme of things—and thus never quite an equal partner in the push-pull of our sartorial neurosis.

Flügel is not alone in assigning primacy to the decorative impulse. Many philosophers of clothing have illuminated a complex matrix of elemental drives that contribute to our desire for self-decoration. These include an innate narcissism and mating behaviors that seek to highlight or exaggerate sexual characteristics. At the deepest level, however, it seems likely that the very first human impulse to cover or alter the body may have originated in the wish to physically attach to oneself an expression of a superstitious or spiritual desire or belief. In other words, talismanic motifs—beginning with body painting, tattooing and scarification, then graduating to amulets, jewelry, and, eventually, clothing—seem as if they may have been the initial expression of our desire to alter, augment, cover, and disguise our bodies. Which means that pretty much everything you can find in a J. Crew catalogue or a Gap outlet can be viewed has having roots in our most primal fetishistic impulses.

I use the word fetishistic, here, in the original sense of the Portuguese *feitiço*, coined by colonizers from that country to denote the objects they noticed West Africans using for religious and magical purposes in the early seventeenth century. *Feitiço* derives from the Latin word *factitious*, which means something created by art—something *artifactual*. The root of *factitious* is the Latin verb *facere*, which means to make or to do. Perhaps it is this etymological consideration that led those who study such things to eventually draw a distinction between sexual obsessions focused on objects and those focused on body parts, since the latter is now officially known as *partialism*. So if you've got a thing for feet you're a partialist, but if you lust after socks, you're a fetishist.

Sock fetishists

On its surface, sock fetishism seems an innocuous quirk. Considering the infinitude of the human imagination and the countless sexual perversions spawned by it, the sock fetishist would appear to be a mild-mannered deviant, a bit silly, perhaps, but no big whoop. After all, what's so bad about loving socks? Fantasizing about socks? Masturbating with socks? Putting socks where socks are not, technically, meant to be put? Who cares? It's nobody's business. Unless it is—because, like any true obsession, sock fetishism can lead to extreme, even criminal behavior, especially as most sock fetishists prefer their goods post-consumer, and for this reason seek out socks that have at some point been on somebody else's feet. Thus they sometimes filch socks—clean but used—from laundry lines, nick them—smelly and sweat-drenched—from locker rooms, and even, occasionally, inveigle them—mid-use—off others' feet.

Some fetishists go to such elaborate lengths to procure their loot that they wind up in jail. One James Dowdy, of Belleville, Missouri, for example, has been arrested over a dozen times, not just for the theft of socks, but for "other types of sock-related incidents," as well, including "using socks in an inappropriate and obscene manner."[6] At times, Dowdy's sock obsession has reached such a state of frenzy that his mother once testified to having occasionally been obliged to chain her middle-aged son to his bed in order to prevent him stealing still more socks. I know there's a lot in that last sentence—a whole novel, maybe—but the point is, sock fetishism isn't always as innocent or silly or nerdy as it may seem on the surface. Like any true passion, it can grow to proportions so outsized as to overshadow one's own existence. As Dowdy once told a judge, "I would like to get help with it so that I can get over it, get it out of my life and get on with my life."[7]

An even stranger case of criminal-level sock fetishism involved two men from Liverpool, Steven Bain and Steven Gawthrop, who, back in the 1990s, managed to con the socks right off the feet of thousands of apparently rather drunk revelers. Their standard procedure was to approach individuals in bars and clubs, and offer them up to £5 for their socks (which, they promised, were going to charity). Bain and Gawthrop were careful to take a photograph of each "donor" and, once back in their shared flat, the men matched the socks to their respective owners' photographs, then stored everything inside plastic zip lock bags. In 1998, both men were found guilty of "conspiring to commit acts of gross indecency." During their hearing, it was revealed that in their raid on Bain and Gawthrop's flat, the police had been obliged to wade through a "carpet" of socks 18 inches deep. "They were all over the furniture, hanging from lampshades and even in the microwave," said one officer. "It was like there had been an explosion in a sock factory." Ultimately, over 4,000 pairs of socks were retrieved from the flat, and although efforts were made to return them to their original owners, not a single pair was reclaimed, so in the end the whole lot actually *was* given to charity. Bain and Gawthrop both served eighteen months for their crimes.[8]

Of course, there are far more innocent sock fetishists out there, and usually it's not such a big deal to get off on socks. It's just a slightly different channel, I think, a little further down the dial, than my maternal fixation on the same garments. What I mean is, in both scenarios, the sock seems desirable or covetable because for some reason it manages to hold onto or absorb a bit of the essence of a person. Maybe Freud was right—maybe the appeal of podophilia and its variants is, at root, smell based, or at least sweat based. Maybe sweat somehow animates a sock, imbues it with something almost life-like—*almost* being a key factor here, because, in the end, the true fetishist is a little afraid of life, and the fact that the fetish itself is merely life-*like* accounts for a large part of its appeal.

In her introduction to the anthology *Fetishism in Fashion*, Lidewij Edelkoort writes, "The fetish is a tool that is able to guide our needs into other territories, such as avoiding a fear of sexual organs by imposing a guardian that will help the transition from reality into fantasy." This "tool," the fetish, becomes a kind of surrogate that allows a person to quell an overwhelming but frightening desire, while at the same time bypassing the true object of that desire because, presumably, the true object is a whole person, with all the soft, bright, and scary bits, the demanding bits, the human bits. This is why Martin, Tournier's protagonist in "The Fetishist," is ultimately compelling—frustrating, yes (he throws away his entire life for the pursuit of "frillies"), and ridiculous, too, but also sympathetic because he is clearly afraid of real women and so must deal instead with mere emanations of them as recorded on the thinnest and smallest possible scraps of fabric.

But if a fetish is a stand-in for another person, what are we to make of the most frightening sock fetishist of all? A man who had no interest in other people's socks, but who loved only his own, and loved them best of all when they when they were brand new? This would be Ted Bundy, the infamous serial killer connected to the murders of at least thirty-six women (although he claimed to have killed nearly three times that number). Yes, Bundy, of all people, was a keen sock fetishist, so keen he actually stole a number of credit cards shortly before his arrest for the purpose of buying himself new athletic socks. His dream was to own so many socks that he'd be able to don a fresh pair each day of the year. Once he confessed, "I am really *sick* when it comes to socks. . . . Socks are such a serious part of my life. They're so very important to me."[9] It strikes me as curious and somehow illuminating (although illuminating of what, exactly, I can't pinpoint) that the sock fetishism of a psychopath like Bundy should attach itself not to socks previously worn by some adored or adorable person, socks that have magically absorbed some special quintessence of that person, but instead to socks of the most pristine and unsullied description, destined only for the killer's own feet.

The psychology of partialism—a thought

The first functional clothes humans ever wore were the animal skins our ancestors sewed together in order to create the warm pseudo-hides that helped them survive the extreme temperatures of the ice age and the migration into the northern reaches of Europe. Though no examples have survived, this type of clothing would presumably have been somewhat formfitting—the better for insulation. For example, it's possible that furs enclosed each leg separately (as Otzi's famous breeches do, although those are eons more recent), and perhaps they even fit the torso closely as well. In other words, the shapes of those very first clothes were likely to have reflected, in some way, human anatomy.

But when we learned the art of weaving, a new kind of clothing emerged. The first garments associated with cloth are called "gravitational" because they hang from the body. Think about it: the toga descends from the shoulders, the cloak from the neck, the loincloth from the waist. . . . For centuries after the advent of weaving, gravitational clothing was the norm because the idea of slicing a hand-woven length of cloth into pieces so as to better fit the body (as necessitated by the act of tailoring: a word that stems from the French *tailler*, meaning "to cut"), would have been unthinkable since cloth, as an object, was far too valuable, in and of itself, to waste in this way. But then, in the Middle Ages, economies of surplus began to emerge. And in economies of surplus there is, of course, surplus—extra to go around. Waste, all of a sudden, became an option, one that gave room for new creative expressions and inventions, among other things. Today, in most modernized countries, tailored, anatomically structured clothing is pretty much a given, and practically everything we wear fits a specific body part: pants fit our legs, shirts fit our arms and torsos, underpants fit our bottoms, bras fit our breasts, gloves fit each individual finger, and socks fit our feet. It all seems a bit fussy, really. I mean, cummerbunds? Tube tops? Dickies?

Since learning about the difference between gravitational and anatomical clothing, I sometimes wonder whether the various shapes and structures of the latter might define and restrict—in a sense fracture—the way we think of our bodies today. In a world full of anatomical clothing, is it possible that we more readily see ourselves as a collection of parts rather than as whole beings? Did the ancient Greeks, for instance, or the ancient Nubians, for that matter, or the ancient Cherokees, know their bodies to be somehow more complete, more perfect, more whole than we understand ours to be today? Impossible to know, perhaps, but this much is true: the first known mention of foot partialism dates back to the writings of Bertold of Regensburg, in a time (1220 CE) and place (Germany) where anatomical clothing was just beginning to emerge in earnest.

Schiele's feet

Egon Schiele—the Austrian Expressionist best known for his contorted self-portraits, and the raw, erotically electrified, sometimes pornographic nudes he painted of women and girls—worked in interesting ways with body parts of all kinds, especially the extremities: arms, legs, hands, and feet. Even hair, in Schiele's work, becomes a kind of extremity, a gesticulating fringe. Schiele's compositions relentlessly break the natural line of the human form, either through the depiction of bizarrely angular postures, by way dramatic croppings, or by simply leaving body parts unpainted. Hands and feet are often summarily rounded off, toes and fingers clipped, at times entire limbs mysteriously disappear into the mottled voids that provide the backdrops of his nudes and portraits. The result is that his subjects often seem to be brusquely abandoned, mid-thought, by the artist; in some instances there's a blatant suggestion of physical amputation, and there are even a handful of drawings and paintings in which every extremity has gone missing, and yet somehow the *idea* of extremities—the reaching-ness of the human body—remains intact. Perhaps nowhere is this more evident than in a self-portrait from 1910 in which the artist's stacked pelvis, trunk, and knob-like head twist themselves into being out of a weird, white-limned void, a composition that calls to mind nothing so much as a tree that's been brutally pruned.

The hands of Schiele's subjects are famous for being bizarre. Twisted, hyper-extended digits communicate fierce but oddly unspecified emotion. Expressive without being eloquent, energized, yet without intent, they speak a body language beyond gesture. Frequently blackened at the tips and spastically splayed, the hands of Schiele's subjects imply disease and/or filth, and ultimately indicate unbearable suffering—an agony of somatic nihilism. Generally speaking, the upper bodies of his nudes tend to echo these qualities, and they are often more flamboyantly twisted and distorted than the lower parts. Particularly in the portraits of women, we find legs that seem passive, heavy, or docile compared to the goings-on of the upper body. Even when thighs are spread wide to expose inflamed genitals, the legs themselves retain an animal gentleness. And yet it's often at the ends of those legs—with the feet—that something really interesting happens.

Schiele's work is flamboyant in its cynicism, theatrical in its ugliness, I think because both cynicism and ugliness seemed to have functioned, for him, as a mode of love: an absolute acceptance of human suffering.

I've been fascinated by Schiele's work ever since I first saw it in an exhibit the Museum of Modern Art (MOMA) put on in the late eighties. I remember standing for a long time—maybe an hour—in front of his 1918 masterpiece, *The Family*, in which a man squats behind a woman, and a woman squats behind (or around) a very young child. The three figures are connected emotionally by their proximity and their nakedness (the child is clothed, but the adults are not), yet at the same time they all seem to float on slightly different pictorial planes, an effect amplified by the fact that each one is looking in a different direction. The skin tones, as is so often the case in Schiele's work, are blotchy—the three of them could be ill, or the light might just be unflattering. Nevertheless, the couple is very beautiful; their features are fine, intelligent, sensitive. The baby is less pretty: it has the uncanny, doll-like quality Schiele sometimes imposed on his sitters. Its eyes are large black buttons—cute, but a little grotesque. The man's anatomy is strange, too; if you look closely, his left leg is far too long. But the thing that struck me the most, even way back then, when I was in college, was the feet: there aren't any. There are three figures. There are six legs. But there are no feet.

There's so much going on in this painting, the lack of feet can seem almost an oversight. The man's direct gaze, for example, is hypnotically intent, while the woman's sidelong glance implies a gentle sadness. The baby, though a bit creepy, is creepy in an innocuous sort of way, if that makes sense. Schiele really got the curve of its cheek right, and that curve, like a chubby close parenthesis, echoes the double curve of the mother's left calf and arm, which, in turn, echoes the double curve of the father's left calf and arm. The figures are nested, almost like Matryoshka dolls, and the spaces they create to hold one another are full of tenderness. But then there's the business of those feet, or lack thereof. The man's feet seem, at first, as if they just happen to be hidden from view, since his left foot is quite pointedly covered by a pile of crumpled white bed sheets and the right is tucked behind the woman. But the woman's feet really aren't there. Her right foot *might* be obscured by something—maybe part of the baby's outfit or the corner of a blanket—it's hard to say. But on the left, her calf just ends. Where we expect to see a foot, there is merely a wash of rust-colored paint, and above that, a rounded stub. Likewise, the baby's feet are simply gone. This lack of feet gives the group a magical, dreamlike, ungrounded quality. It makes one nervous for them. They seem too vulnerable. Trapped, immobilized. Above all, resigned.

Schiele's socks

Most of Schiele's nudes are not entirely nude. Instead, the model might wear a skirt (although it may be upturned), a rumpled petticoat, a slipping slip, an unbuttoned shirt . . . . And even in those nudes that are truly—which is to say, fully—nude, the skin tones often shift wildly from body part to body part, implying hands gloved in gangrene, chests corseted by sexual flush, bellies girdled by eczema, grunge, or bruises. . . . By far the most common piece of clothing worn (or chromatically implied) in Schiele's nudes and semi-nudes are socks and stockings, which make an appearance in over 100 drawings and paintings. I admit I arrived at this figure through the rather unscientific method of repeated Google image searches involving different combinations of the words "Schiele" "socks" "stockings" "nudes" "portraits," and "feet," but I'd bet good money that a more formal survey would actually put the number significantly higher.

In Schiele's work, we find women wearing jade-green stockings and women wearing pine-green stockings, women wearing turquoise-blue stockings, and women wearing olive-colored stockings. There are many, many, many black socks on both men and women. There's one especially notable emerald-colored anklet on a woman's foot poised just over her crotch. There are striped socks and plaid socks and mustard-yellow socks, red stockings, and orange stockings and brown stockings. Some socks slip down the calves to the ankles, others are held up on the thighs by bows. Sometimes the artist has left the feet unpainted, yet taken care to depict the upper cuff of a sock or stocking—the merest hint of fabric—as if to indicate the amorphous borders of a ghost-limb. There are gray stockings and striped stockings and grid-patterned stockings, and there is one pair of stockings in the most beautiful shade of blue (dark, chalky) I may have ever seen. Then there are those socks that aren't socks at all, just cold skin or hot skin or dirty skin or diseased skin. And what I want to know is, what the hell was he doing with all these socks? All these stockings?

At least one critic has claimed that in Schiele's work stockings "are used fetishistically to heighten a sense of sexual fantasy,"[10] but I think this is oversimplifying things. Johann Nepomuk Geiger—now there's a guy who used socks fetishistically in his work. But Schiele's socks are at least as sad as they are sexy. They're somber, in fact. Take, for example, one of the many portraits he made of himself masturbating, the one in which he wraps his arms across his chest, and stands with his legs spread to reveal a penis so quiescent it looks like a small tulip. Outside of the title, *Masturbation*, there is no way to know that the man in this picture has been engaged in the act of onanism, except, perhaps—yes, there's something in his face: a flushed cheek, an open mouth. It's a face gently smeared by private oblivion. Not surprisingly, his lower legs and feet are cropped from the composition. One thigh balloons gently toward the bottom edge of the painting, cut off at the knee. The other leg is bent and lifted toward the viewer. This leg occupies both the foreground and the lower left quadrant of the work, and it is encased in the blackest possible blackness: a completely opaque field. There is no hint of texture to imply fabric, no contours to speak of. It could almost be a stain: a puddle of spilled ink, and yet a stocking is clearly signified—one so long as to hint at belonging to a woman. The intense blackness of this shape weighs the image down, unbalances the composition, threatens to destroy it. The image as a whole only manages to achieve an awkward harmony thanks to the artist's hair, at the top edge of the painting: a thick, spiky crown of equally intense black. Between these two poles (to borrow Bataille's terms) are stretched the subtle, furless shades of human flesh—mostly pinks in this case, and slightly grimy: soft, muscled, sinuous. But the blackness at either end is so black as to suggest an encroaching void— something inhuman, absolute. So, no, I don't think Schiele used socks and stockings merely to "heighten sexual fantasy." His socks may be sexy. But they're not about sex.

This is not to say that his work as a whole isn't sexual. Schiele was supremely alert to the carnal aspect of every element of the human body, which, interestingly, kind of puts him out of the running for partialism. After all, if *everything* is sexualized—shoulder blades, fingernails, eyelids—then even a vulva painted in the most blaring of reds achieves a raunchiness that can only be called egalitarian.

The sole's soul

In *The Sex Life of Foot and Shoe*, William Rossi insists that the foot, so "rich with vibratory and electromagnetic powers," is responsible for "the voluptuous architecture of the body," an architecture that makes possible frontally oriented copulation ("a coital position unique in all nature").[11] Desmond Morris, in *The Naked Ape*, wonders, "Could our vertical posture have influenced our sexual signals?" He then answers his own question with a resounding yes, mostly because of the fact that "virtually all the sexual signals and erogenous zones are on the front of the body—the facial expressions, the lips, the beard, the nipples, the areolar signals, the breasts of the female, the pubic hair, the genitals themselves, the major blushing areas, and the major sexual flush areas."[12]

Just as our feet contain more sweat glands than seems quite possible (250,000), so do they hold more nerve endings, per square centimeter, than any other part of the human body—some suggest as many as seven or eight thousand per foot. We need all this feedback in order to maintain our balance because we are constantly adjusting our entire systems to the subtlest gradations of the surface beneath us in order not to fall, as standing on two feet is an activity that requires constant neurological monitoring. If you want to test the sensitivity of your feet for yourself, notice how alive they feel the next time the lights suddenly go out. At a moment like this, if you pay attention, you'll find the entire plantar surfaces of both feet buzzing madly, searching for information to keep you upright.

The great number of nerves in the soles of our feet explains why they are so ticklish. It also explains the practice of *bastinado*, or caning the soles as a form of punishment or torture, and perhaps it also has something to do with the fact that, in Chinese medicine, the foot is used as a "microsystem," with each toe, each toe pad, the different sections of heel, mid-, and fore-foot, corresponding to some larger part of the soma floating above.

The incredible sensitivity of our feet is the most commonsense explanation for podophilia, as well as for far simpler pleasures, such as the *hyggeligt* luxury of slipping one's feet into a pair of warm, soft socks on a cold winter's day. Socks, incidentally, are very good for sex, especially if you're a woman. At least, one study has found that women achieved orgasm significantly more readily while wearing them. The scientists who conducted this study used electromagnetic imaging to track those areas of the brain most active during sex, and, based on those images, they found that women wearing socks were far more receptive to signals of arousal than those not wearing socks, perhaps (the scientists conjectured) because the warmth and comfort provided by socks served to calm the entire nervous system.[13]

Yet socks also cut us off from sensual experience. A perfect example of anatomical clothing, the sock fits the foot like a second skin, but it is not skin, it is fabric, and as such it hinders the ability of our feet to fully feel and respond to our environment, just as gloves hinder the ability of our hands to do the same.

Our feet are plantigrade, meaning the entire plantar aspect, or sole, makes contact with the ground. This is unlike the foot of a cat, for instance, or a dog, both of which have feet that are skeletally arranged in a kind of permanent tiptoe formation, with the heel arched high over the toes. It is only because our feet are plantigrade that we are truly bipedal, since we use of the entire length of the foot, at different phases of the gait cycle, as both a platform and a propulsive lever. We are not the only plantigrade mammals, but we are the only plantigrade mammals that rise up from our feet and stay there—like vegetal forms, like trees, as Bataille suggests.

No doubt it is because our feet have such complete contact with the ground on which they stand that both prefixes associated with them—*ped-* and *pod-* —are related to the Greek word *pedon*, which means "soil" or "ground." Our word *sole* comes from the Latin *solum*, which also means "soil" or "ground." These etymological roots clearly reflect the foot's special relationship to the earth.

Health enthusiasts have long maintained that the sole of the bare foot is designed to absorb emanations from the planet itself, energy that has the ability to heal and feed the human body and spirit. In a 1914 pamphlet entitled *The Barefoot League: Being a Tête a Tête on the Virtues and Delights of Barefoot Walking, between You and Your Brother in Life*, James Leith Macbeth Bain claimed that "it is through the soles of the feet that humans receive the finest of the sun's energy [and] also the virtues of the body of our earth in all its manifold richness and power." In her essay "The Modern Foot," Janet Lyon summarizes Bain's argument this way: "The sole of the foot is . . . both a nutritional and a spiritual membrane; to deny contact between the foot and the earth is to ensure the deformation of body and soul."[14]

As far-fetched as this idea may seem, recent studies from the National Institutes for Health confirm it, and a new trend, called "earthing" is currently growing in popularity. Earthing consists, in part, of walking barefoot over unpaved ground in order to heal, alleviate or avoid such problems as insomnia, stress, chronic pain, and osteoporosis, among others.[15] Since learning about this practice, I—health nut that I kind of, sort of am—have started to spend a little time each day walking around outside barefoot, weather permitting. In the Boston suburb where I live it's not easy to find a patch of bare earth, but it's not impossible. There's a playing field on my block and I try to walk or run a couple of times around its grassy circumference every day (although I try not to do so when my son is playing there with friends). I can't say with certainty whether I'm soaking up any especially good vibes through my feet, but I can tell you this: I find something *grounding* about earthing. At least, it seems to me that barefoot contact with that patchy grass helps me feel just a little more centered. Calmer. Somehow more horizontal, if that makes sense.

Sparkling brainworlds

Georges Bataille would have disagreed with my hypothesis about tailored clothes and psychic dislocation. He thought human anatomy itself was to blame for our fractured sense of self, not our clothing. According to him, the unique verticality of our structure, stretched between earth and sky, is essentially unnatural, deformed, and the result of this defect is a constant short-circuiting of impulses on both sexual and spiritual fronts. The only possible solution, Bataille suggests in a fragmentary note related to his essay "The Pineal Eye," is to *accentuate* the problem. "It is necessary to break oneself in pieces and feel in one's body the madness of a contortionist; at the same time one must become a fetishist to the point of slavering, a fetishist of the eye, of the buttocks and of the feet, all at once, in order to find again in oneself what miserably miscarried at the beginning of the constitution of the human body."[16]

It's not much of a reach to find in Schiele's work—with its relentless twistings, amputations, and spastic gesticulations—a fairly accurate illustration of Bataille's logic. The nudes in particular seem to insist that we humans are intrinsically broken, physiologically confused. There are hints, as well, of this same metaphysics of disorder in Schiele's more formal portraits and, even, in his landscapes. In fact, nowhere is it more apparent, I think, than in the leafless trees Schiele painted in 1911 and 1912: solitary arboreal beings that, with their painfully arched and zigzagging limbs, bear a striking resemblance to his nudes. I am not the first to notice the personification of these trees, but I may be the first to notice that they are wearing socks. Not the same kind of socks worn by Anne Sexton's trees (each branch of which, after snow, sports "the sock of God")—no, Schiele's trees wear long plain stockings of limewash that stretch upward from the ground to cover almost the entire length of their trunks. Much like the black stocking in *Masturbation*, these white areas serve, graphically, to sever each subject from the ground on which it stands, or, rather, out of which it emerges. Divorced from the earth, and thus from their own roots, the limbs of these trees stretch, jaggedly, against a pale sky, looking—to my eye at least—less like the branches of trees than the synapses of a brain.

—

The word "desire" stems from the Latin words *de* (meaning "of") and *sidere* (meaning "stars"). Desire, in other words, is a thing "of the stars." But what does that mean? Are we talking "unreachable" or are we talking "glittering"? Or does "of the stars" simply mean distant?

Egon Schiele wasn't just a painter, he also wrote poetry—not a lot, but enough to be illuminating. In his poem, "Sun," he insists, like Bataille, that the sky is where we keep our heads. "Gaze at stars yellow and glittering," he urges, "till you feel good and have to shut out the blinking. / Brainworlds sparkle in your caves." Interestingly, the you in "Sun" is described as being "thirsty and tottering." Thirsty, I get—desire is often associated with it. But why "tottering"? Does desire—that sidereal temptress—so imbalance us?

But what about my subject: the sock? I promise I haven't left that humble little foot-sweater behind, that porous pouch—so useful, in a pinch, for all sorts of things: makeshift mittens or floppy dolls or cheapo draft stoppers. With the help of an old sock, you can diffuse the stream of air from a blow dryer to keep your curls intact, or wipe up a puddle of come, or cushion your Christmas tree ornaments for safe storage, or increase the size of your "package" by stuffing it into your pants. You can even make a fairly effective weapon out of a sock if you fill it with sand, nails, or coins, and take good aim. A sock makes a decent tourniquet, an okay change purse, a funny puppet, a pretty good duster, and—oh, irony of ironies—a handy shoe-protector when traveling. . . . It is really a very useful thing, although some podiatrists warn that our socks are just as responsible as our shoes for the deformation of the human foot, since socks inhibit the naturally spatulate spread of our toes (just as mittens inhibit the full range of our fingers). On top of that, even the thinnest and most threadbare of socks will interrupt the transmission of the planet's electromagnetic energies to our sensitive soles. In fact, pulling on a pair of socks is, for many people, the first act of the day that serves to divorce them from their sleepy, horizontal, animal-selves, because socks raise the body up from the terrestrial plane, however infinitesimally, and in this way tip the scales just that much more in favor of stars and brainworlds, dreams and desires. Yes, indeed, no matter how mundane the sock as an object may be, its function is, ultimately, to make *us* less so.

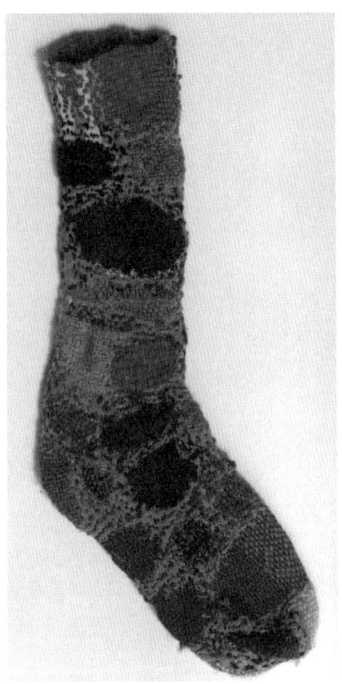

FIGURE 3 Darned sock by artist Celia Pym. From *first one's the best* (detail), 60 sports socks, wool and acrylic yarn, 2015. Photo Credit: Michele Panzeri. Courtesy of the artist.

3 SOCKS AND INDUSTRY

I'm not sure how I got here, in the weird little warrens of sock ontology, hosiery history. It's a strange place, to be sure, although I guess I'm not too surprised that I've landed here, given my love of small things—small, domestic things. Cookies and houseplants and children's clumsy art projects, books and pillows, frying pans and baskets of onions, of fruit, of potatoes, a bag of birdseed, a pile of laundry . . . . The details of our homes speak a special language, the primary structures of which are rooted in our attitudes toward comfort and complacency, desire and resignation, habit, apathy, and that particular brand of industry we call "keeping." My own home, to be honest, is a bit of mess, but it's a good home, even if it's not very large or fancy. In fact, it's rather small and down at the heels, and, as one friend recently put it, "materially dense," which I think just means full of stuff.

The language of the home is generally mumbled, but with an accent. The accent is feminine because the home has traditionally been the domain, the *domus*, of women. This may be changing, shifting as gender roles continue shift. Or it may be that our homes themselves are changing—becoming less home-like as ever larger portions of our lives, even the most intimate aspects, flatten and attenuate in order to accommodate the digital oscillations of our screens and the various social media projected onto them. In any case, a certain shame remains attached to the idea of *keeping house*, no doubt because, at least in Western cultures, a far greater value has historically been placed on the activities performed outside the home than on those performed inside it. Even feminists have largely subscribed to this devaluation of what has been, for millennia, the arena of women's primary contributions to the species. Perhaps this was a necessary betrayal of our foremothers, made in order to pry open doors that needed opening, beginning with the one at the front of the house. But it still seems unfair. Ungrateful. Disrespectful. And, ultimately, shortsighted.

In his essay "House for Sale," Jonathan Franzen writes, of his mother, "Her home was the heavy (but not infinitely heavy) and sturdy (but not everlasting) God that she'd loved and served and been sustained by." I know that God. No—no, I don't. Not really. But in my home I *have* noticed something Godlike, if you think of God as a kind of spore, maybe. Or something like pollen. A kind of dense, super-saturated, vast but invisible dust. I don't know what this thing is, exactly, is but I do know that it seems to be more concentrated in some objects than in others. For example, it seems to cling with particular tenacity to my husband's bifocals. And socks. Sometimes it clings to socks.

Sock as home

A sock is many things. A sack for the foot. A foot condom. A pediform sheath. A buffer. An insulator. A sweat sponge. A smell lodger. A bit of flash. A suggestion of sex. A magnet for holes. Above all, a wanderer. But technically speaking, a sock is really just "an inner foot covering," and, as such, it can only truly fulfill its function when accompanied by an "outer foot covering." Normally this is a shoe or a boot. Between the outer and the inner foot coverings, the outer is usually considered the more essential, which is why we say, "Put on your shoes and socks!" instead of, "Put on your socks and shoes!" This actually has a name. It's what's known as a *hysteron proteron*: a rhetorical device that reverses the temporal order of an event so as to give primacy to the more significant element. But when it comes to shoes and socks, that order can get complicated pretty quickly because there are, generally speaking, two of both things, and our private protocols for getting all four items onto our feet before we go out into the world reflects something of how we, as individuals, negotiate the transition between the home and the larger world, as illustrated by the following debate between Archie Bunker and his son-in-law Michael (a.k.a. "Meathead"), in a 1974 episode of *All in the Family*:

Archie (in disbelief, having just watched a barefoot Michael put on a sock and then, on the same foot, a shoe): Don't you know that the whole *world* puts on a sock and a sock and a shoe and a shoe?

Michael: I like to take care of one foot at a time.

A: That's the *dumbest* thing I ever heard in my life.

M: It's just as quick my way.

A (increasingly angry): Wait a minute. That ain't the point. . . . Suppose there's a fire in the house and you gotta run for your life? Your way, all you got on is one shoe and a sock. My way, you got on a sock and a sock. You see, you're even?

M: Suppose it's raining or snowing outside. Your way, with a sock on each foot, my feet would get wet. My way, with a sock and a shoe on one foot, I could hop around and stay dry.

A: I think you been hoppin' around on your head. . . . Supposin' the other sock has a hole in it?

M (nonplussed): It doesn't have a hole in it.

A (impatient): I said *supposin'* it has a hole in it. All right, it has a hole in it. So, you ain't got another matching pair, so what are you gonna do? Your way, you gotta take off the whole shoe and the sock. My way, all you gotta do is take off one sock.

M: All right. If it'll make you happy, I'll start all over again.

I'm not sure what it says about me, but to this day I retain a vivid memory of watching this episode as a kid, and thinking, "Wow. They *both* have good points!"

—

J. C. Flügel wrote that clothes, "like the house, are protective, but, being nearer the body and actually supported on it, they are (unlike the house) portable. With their help, we carry—like snails and tortoises—a sort of home upon our backs."[1] In a similar vein, Bernard Rudofsky, in his 1947 book-length essay *Are Clothes Modern?*, describes the "seven veils of the male stomach," which run (from inner to outer): undershirt; drawers; shirt; trousers; vest; coat; and overcoat.[2] Equivalents can easily be imagined for women and those sartorial daredevils, the non- or differently gendered. In all cases, the physically and psychologically protective qualities of clothing are such that it is only when our entire arsenal of "veils" is in place that we find ourselves perfectly equipped to meet both meteorological and social challenges. But with removal of each layer, we are required to seek tighter and tighter circles of architectural protection and social intimacy. When wearing nothing but the innermost veils (which consist, at the lower altitudes, of socks and stockings), we, as a rule, feel safe only in the private domain. Simply put, socks worn alone and out of doors are a disruption of the natural order of things. I suppose this explains why they're capable of reaching such special heights of awkwardness. Yet at home, a sock is perfectly *at* home.

Fast fashion

Socks, of course, are but one element of our human wardrobe. We wear pants and shirts and shorts and dresses, sweaters, hats, coats, boots, shoes, gloves, underwear, scarves, hoodies, and gowns. Also: ponchos, saris, thermals, leggings, pj's, aprons, jumpsuits, business suits, shawls, vests, jackets, parkas, blazers, and raincoats, to name only some of the more common items.

According to one of its giants, Eileen Fisher, the clothing industry as a whole is the second dirtiest in the world, with oil being the first.[3] Estimates for the amount of water used by annual worldwide fiber and textile production range from 1.5 to 2 trillion gallons. And post-production those gallons are very often poisoned with unsafe levels of toxins, such as lead and mercury, making the apparel industry the second largest polluter of fresh water globally. On top of this, 10 percent of the world's total carbon footprint can be attributed to it.[4]

Numbers like these climb steadily every day, thanks not only to our ever-increasing population, but to the phenomenon known as "fast fashion," which has raised the traditional cycles of fashion from between two and four times a year, to somewhere between eleven and fifteen, or even more.[5] Fast fashion is not only fast, it's disposable, being generally so poorly made its products often fall apart at the seams after just a handful of wearings. But this hardly matters to consumers, because fast fashion cycles through trends with incredible rapidity, in large part because there is little to no expectation of keeping the clothes for more than a year or so. This means that our clothing problems aren't only on the manufacturing end of things, but on the disposal end as well. Landfills are clogged with old clothes—or, rather, with new clothes that nobody wants to wear any more. To complicate matters, the majority of our clothes are made with some type of non-organic material. Polyester alone can be found in over 50 percent of our clothing, which is bad because polyester is a plastic and as such doesn't degrade for hundreds of years.

Because it's so cheap, and because it changes so quickly and is disposed of so thoughtlessly, fast fashion has upped clothing consumption 400 percent compared to two decades ago.[6] Not surprisingly, Americans buy more clothes than people from other countries, with the average US citizen purchasing sixty-eight new articles of clothing every year[7] and throwing away about eighty-two pounds of textiles annually.[8] "Buy and chuck" seems to be our method—if you can call the rapacious, media-hypnotized, and seemingly mindless activity of our late capitalist consumerism a "method." But this is hardly news. We know this story. We've been in this handbasket for ages. Yet for some reason we remain unable to stop ourselves from gobbling up natural resources and spitting out pollutants. There's plastic lint in every waterway, and slavery (though it goes by other names and is conveniently hidden from first world consumers) is alive and well under the aegis of global economics. Maybe we just don't want to change. Or maybe real change is actually impossible. After all, how do you put the brakes on 7.4 billion people? How do you tame the appetites of the wealthiest of those people when information itself is a commodity, and our votes count for less than our dollars?

#Sockgame

Fashion is a mode of desire. We don't need fashion, we *want* fashion. Clothes are sometimes a necessity, but fashionable clothes are things we *like* to have, to wear for the sake of wearing, or perhaps for the sake of showing off, since the more fashionable the outfit, the more we hope to express things like power, prestige, and sexual appeal.

Although fashion may be the product of desire, it "experiences itself as a Right, the natural right of the present over the past"[9] because "every year fashion destroys that which it has just been admiring, and adores that which it is about to destroy."[10] These lines are from Roland Barthes' *The Language of Fashion*, a collection of writings in which he makes a strong—actually, pretty much an airtight—case for fashion being, above all, an act of communication.

Fashion, Barthes argues, constitutes a complex system of symbols—a language whose words and grammar are made up of clothes and the ways in which we wear them. We exchange signals with one another using our clothes in order to convey information such as our social status, our sexual availability, our level of education, our general worldliness, and our mood of the day, among other things. And one of the most crucial ways that our clothes allow us to communicate with one another is by way of the all-important *detail*, the "next-to-nothing," the "*je ne sais quois.*"

According to Barthes, the role of the detail expanded in the aftermath of the French Revolution, when the rise of democratic ideals made it unseemly for men, in particular, to dress in the more old-fashioned mode, a mode that employed actual costumes to delineate individual occupations, social roles, and status. Instead, the business suit, plain and buttoned up ("essentially from the Quaker model"), became the egalitarian outfit of choice. But because the classes themselves were far from abolished, "clothing had to cheat." Details—"the knot on a cravat, the material of a shirt, the buttons on a waistcoat, the buckle on a shoe"—became the only reliable way to communicate one's place within the social pecking order. Using details, men sidestepped the stringent dress code of the democratic impulse by asserting something called "individual taste."

Women have never been beholden in quite the same way to vestiary democracy, in large part because of what, until relatively recently, has been their financial dependence upon men. Indeed, the opulence of women's clothing often operated much like "the buckle of a shoe," meaning that the beauty of a woman's outfit could (and still can: Melania) point directly to the status of the man who bought and provided it. But with no women nearby to advertise the state of their finances, men are generally obliged to distinguish themselves, sartorially, through tiny gestures, or, in Barthes' lingo, *vestemes*. And these days, the most potent *vesteme* that a man of at least moderate means might opt to employ is a pair of richly pattered, colorful, humorous, or unusually textured socks.

Socks have always lent themselves to decoration. In fact, the very first true-knit socks we know of—the so-called "Coptic socks"—are striking examples of graphic design: blue-on-white geometric and floral patterns interspersed with lines of Kufic script. As the form of the sock evolved, so did the art of its decoration, and in the nineteenth century the socks and stockings of the upper classes in Europe reached what would seem to be the height of decorative glory, with ankle gores (called "clocks") embroidered with colorful silks in elaborate designs that might include birds, flowers, fruits, and elegant geometries, despite the fact that many of these stunning creations were often hidden under long gowns.

But today, thanks to computer-aided design, the decorations on our socks go beyond even this. Today, our socks sometimes tell whole stories, as is the case with a pair I own (probably my favorite) that show a clumsily drawn woman in a red dress pushing a huge rock with a smiley face on it up the steep incline of a snow-covered mountain. Scrawled across the instep: "Well, this sucks." Jokes are a big part of socks these days. Consider, for example, the pair you can get for $5.98 from Walmart that are covered with clouds, and that implore, on the calf, "Look within," then add, on the foot, "the fridge."

There are socks printed all over with Marilyn Monroe's face, and socks printed all over with fried eggs, and socks printed all over with Da Vinci's *Mona Lisa*. There are transparent socks embroidered with realistic renderings of wild mushrooms in very fine silk thread, and socks made of a dozen different fabrics and textures, and socks that boast migraine-inducing combinations of stripes, circles, and zigzags. There are socks that depict charming pastoral scenes, or dusty Western ghost towns, or the entire solar system. And even though men still wear the kinds of suits Barthes described as "Quaker," such puritanical conformity no longer applies to the male foot and ankle. Yes, the male foot and ankle are stepping out. The male foot and ankle are expressing—something. I'm just not sure what. Individuality? Maybe, but if so, why is the #sockgame, as it's called on social media, so overwhelmingly popular? #Sockgame being the hashtag you use if you want to brag about your socks and post pictures of them on Twitter or Instagram.

Many of the most popular #sockgame socks are topical in nature. Novelty items. For instance, you can get a pair of socks with a particular baseball player's face emblazoned on the ankle if you're going to a game and want to root for him. Or you can get a pair of socks decorated with a political slogan; and these function as pins used to, in part because they are just as cheaply made and thoughtlessly disposed of. There are socks for every season and every day of the week, and you can buy socks for specific holidays, even very strange holidays, like National Ice Cream Sandwich Day and National Lighthouse Day. Thanks to fast fashion, socks, being cheap to begin with, have only gotten more so, and the interval between purchase and disposal would seem to be very narrow indeed in some cases, particularly with novelty socks, such as those that feature a thick, 3-D orange acrylic thatch of fluff sticking off of Donald Trump's forehead.

Slow fashion

The opposite of fast fashion is slow fashion, which, like slow food, advocates quality over convenience and sustainability over profit. Made by hand, often locally, using organic materials and ecologically sound production methods, slow fashion tends to be very expensive, which is why (again, like slow food) many of its adherents are also practitioners, meaning, they make their own clothes. Because it's a lot cheaper to make slow clothes than it is to buy slow clothes. Which isn't the same thing as saying "cheap." Take knitting, for example. I've knit a fair number of sweaters and the least expensive one cost me $45 in yarn alone. I think that's about as little as you can expect to get away with if you're making a sweater for an adult. I'm talking about wool, of course; polyester might be cheaper, but then you're no longer making something slow.

On top of materials, there's also the time needed to complete a knitting project, and you know what time is. Practically nobody knits by hand for a living anymore, so it's become a hobby, a leisure time activity. You can't knit a sweater by hand if you're working two jobs. For this reason, the products of slow fashion are inevitably (though often subtly) emblems of conspicuous consumption, only what's being consumed aren't obvious goods and services, but time and the opportunities it creates. And what's on display isn't explicitly monetary wealth so much as a kind of privilege—not necessarily white, but almost certainly liberal, educated, and philosophically righteous (or PC, take your pick). Slow fashion also tends to exude a kind of willful innocence fed by a nostalgic yearning for better, "simpler" times.

In this last respect, slow fashion reflects an interesting side of the domestic arts—something Marie Antoinette highlighted with her miniature hamlet built on the grounds of Versailles: eleven peasant cottages with eleven kitchen gardens surrounded by eleven hornbeam hedges. In Hameau de la Reine, the queen and her companions pretended to be milkmaids. Who knows, maybe they even darned a stocking or two? But just outside the castle grounds, real peasants were starving to death and the revolution was mounting. What I'm getting at is this: there's something about the pursuit of the domestic arts that inspires the romantically inclined—but only if that pursuit is optional. Nobody wants to be poor enough to *need* to be a milkmaid, or to *have* to make their own clothes. But if you *want* to make your own clothes—well, that's another matter entirely.

That time I made a sock

Last year, I decided to knit my daughter a pair of socks. Although I love knitting, knitting socks has always struck me as a daunting task, which is why I signed up for a how-to class called, appropriately enough, "Knitting Socks." This class took place at a yarn store not far from my house and, at first, there were ten of us students, but we quickly dwindled to four—though I suppose such attrition is to be expected when the task at hand is not only small and fiddly but, by turns, both baffling *and* tedious.

On the first day of class, our teacher handed out a pattern of her own design called "Socks Ed." This document was eight pages long, which I found slightly alarming, as I have knit intricate cabled cardigans using patterns of fewer than three pages. But "Socks Ed." is full of explanatory asides, examples, and guidelines, such as:

To determine the correct width of your sock, use your gauge and your foot-width measurement, remembering to calculate that 10% negative ease. Since this is a simple stockingnette stitch sock, you can use virtually any number of stitches, with the following caveats: you begin the sock with a ribbed cuff—if you want k1p1 rib, you need an even number of stitches, and if you want k2p2 rib then you need a multiple of four. Multiples of four will also make the heel a bit easier (because you'll be able to divide the heel and instep stitches evenly), but it's not strictly necessary.[11]

Such information was clearly meant to be helpful, but I found it merely overwhelming. What was helpful, however, was being able to watch the teacher perform the various operations involved in knitting socks. For example, there is a special cast-on technique that makes an especially effective (i.e., clingy yet stretchy) cuff. It's called "Tillybuddy's Very Stretchy Cast-On" and it requires much yarn flipping, loop twisting, and needle transferring. I would never have been able to learn this technique from a book or a video. I needed to watch the teacher's fingers flick through the motions on her many double-pointed needles while I mimicked those motions, slowly and clumsily, but eventually with some success.

For five Sunday mornings in a row, our shrinking group worked together around a narrow table in the middle of the store. Each class lasted about an hour. I knit in a pale, gray-blue yarn that reminded me of my daughter's favorite sweatshirt; I figured she'd like the color. After a few tries, I finally was able to complete Tillybuddy's Very Stretchy Cast-On, and for a while after that, I felt optimistic, because once you get past the cuff of a sock you get to "knit straight" for several inches—and knitting straight on circular needles is a cinch, you just go, go, go. So things seemed peachy for a while. I no longer had to look at each and every stitch I was making and I got to go on knitting auto-pilot, which is always fun. I chatted with my classmates while imagining, in the back of my mind, the drawers I'd soon be filling at home with dozens of hand-knit socks, thick and plush and colorful and full of love. Then I got to the heel. Knitting the heel (or "turning" it, in knitting parlance) is a tricky thing. It's done like this: you put half your stitches aside on a spare needle and keep knitting the remainder. Your goal is to create a kind of cup that will both cover the heel and change the direction of your knitting from vertical (leg) to horizontal (foot), only at first what you're knitting doesn't look anything like a cup, it looks like a flap. In fact, it is a flap—the "heel flap"—which only becomes a heel cup after you pick up the stitches you'd earlier put aside and connect them to it (the flap), by making little triangular gores that take a lot of math. At least, I thought it was a lot of math. It's all quite dramatic, even if it doesn't sound like it, and around our table in the yarn store, there was a lot of sighing and grunting, and scribbling of numbers on scraps of paper. Many stitches were knit, then ripped out, then knit again. Eventually, I managed the full turn. It wasn't pretty. But it wasn't too bad. After the heel came another stretch of straight knitting, which was sweet, and then the tapering of the toe, but that was no big deal. I've tapered plenty of times. The only problem, really, was casting off, which in socks—at least those knit starting from the cuff— is also a matter of closing up the toe. This operation is best done with something called the Kitchener stitch—a rather magical technique that leaves no evidence of its working, and so no seam to speak of. Once again, the teacher walked me through the process—a clever hybrid of knitting and weaving—and, voilà, I'd made a sock! I couldn't believe it: a whole entire sock—gray blue with a bright yellow toe. Then the class ended.

Craftivism

Knitting by hand is a time-consuming activity. It can seem pointless to knit a sweater by hand, let alone a hat, a scarf, or a pair of socks, when such things can be bought so cheaply and quickly—often with little more effort than a keystroke. Perhaps it's for this reason that knitting, despite its current flare of popularity, is still viewed by many as a spinsterish hobby, a dowdy or neurotic occupation, one often depicted—especially in movies—as a cliché of sexual frustration, each stitch a lover lost. Knitting, to the non-knitter, can seem overly concerned with minutiae, an obsessive infatuation with tiny details. In short: a waste of time.

Knitters in literature tend to be a crackpot lot. There's the vengeful Madame Defarge, of course, in Dickens' *A Tale of Two Cities*, with her secret knitted codes of revenge. And Conrad's "old knitter of black wool" in *Heart of Darkness*, who, "uncanny and fateful," seems able to send people to their graves simply by looking at them a certain way from over her silver spectacles. There's the coal-dealer's wife—a "bad woman"—in Kafka's "The Bucket Rider," who refuses a freezing man a handful of coal, insisting she can't hear or see him pleading with her while she calmly knits next to a crackling fire. And there's the wife in Thomas Bernhard's *The Lime Works*, an invalid who knits, unravels, and re-knits the same single mitten for years on end.

What is it about knitting that implies this kind of quiet insanity? Sneaky, steadfast, unflinching, secretly cruel? Perhaps the repetitive actions involved in knitting imply a dangerous level of patience (by my estimation, the last sweater I knit—an oversized white turtleneck for my teenage daughter—required more than 62,000 stitches). Or maybe the negative stereotypes surrounding knitters boil down to basic crone-hatred: a classic mash-up of sexism and ageism. Or maybe they reflect mainstream society's deep suspicion of Luddite tendencies—after all, what kind of person, in this day and age, *chooses* to knit when knitted goods are so easily *bought*? Is there, hidden in the activity, a rejection of commercialism? Of materialism? Of consumerism? Of corporatism? Or any of the other commonly held values reinforced by our industrialized existence?

Actually, yes indeed, there is.

Craftivism is a somewhat amorphous field of activity, generally taken up by a slightly hipper type of knitter than those we know from Dickens, Conrad, and Bernhard. The craftivist knitter is a kind of chipper inversion of the sinister spinster trope. An adherent of all things slow, she (or he) is even kind of cool, in a comfortably nerdy way, yet still surrounded by a nimbus of old-fashioned domestic can-do.

As its name implies, "craftivism" is a combination of crafts plus activism. However the "activist" part of the equation can be pretty subtle, since craftivists take very seriously the idea that the personal *is* the political. So you don't actually have to adorn your socks or your cakes or your 'zines with political slogans to make a strong political statement. Simply taking the time to make something by hand *is* the statement. The time itself, and the skill involved, the human touch: all these things are all evidence of the craftivist's personal (which is to say, political) investment a tangible good. And the very existence of that handmade good—be it a neon-colored embroidery sampler, a jar of pickled strawberries, or a pair of Kool-Aid-dyed socks—serves, in a quiet, self-contained sort of way, as a protest against the corporate hegemony that dictates so many aspects of our material lives. As Faith Gillespie, a well-known craftivist, has put it:

There is clearly another imperative at work now in our exercise of the old crafts. It has to do with reclamation, with reparation. The world seems not to need us anymore to make "the things of life" machines make more and cheap [*sic*]. The system needs us to do the maintenance jobs and to run the machines that produce the so-called "goods," to be machines in the consumer societies which consume and consume and are empty. Our turning to craftwork is a refusal. We may not all see ourselves this way, but we are working from a position of dissent. And that is a political position.[12]

A concrete act

Craftivism seems like a good idea, but—I don't know. My craft-aspirations have always been less lofty than that. I learned to knit, for instance, not for political or ecological reasons, but because I wanted to be a good mother. Like many women, I was terrified of being a bad mother. In my case, this terror was specific; it stemmed from the fact that my own mother is mentally ill and, in the nature of things, had proven a problematic role model when I was growing up. For some reason, I thought that learning to knit would be a concrete act I could take, one that would teach me how to be a different sort of mother altogether: patient, competent, quietly affectionate. These are the things I was going for.

I took my first knitting class when my daughter was an infant. Our assignment, conveniently enough, was to make a baby hat. It was supposed to look like a flower and it was knit, as most hats are (and socks, for that matter), in the round, using several small double-pointed needles. I found these needles frustrating—fussy, tiny, far too numerous. The yarn kept getting tangled up in them, and at the same time they were always slipping out of my fingers. But my biggest problem was that I continually knit into the hat the wrong way. You see, when you knit in the round, rows aren't technically rows at all, but layers of a single spiral, endlessly building upon itself. There is actually a simple trick for keeping your work oriented when knitting in the round, but at the time, I didn't know it, and I was baffled. So baffled, I eventually abandoned the hat in favor of a project I could knit flat—that is, back and forth in proper rows using two long, straight, single-pointed needles. The pattern I chose was for a tiny cardigan, size "6 mos. to 1 yr." The yarn was a bright, almost cherry red wool-angora blend so soft it collapsed like foam under my fingers. Although there were five pieces to that pattern (a back, a left front, a right front, a left sleeve, a right sleeve), I found it much more straightforward than the cap, and in the end that cardigan was a great success—a little lopsided, maybe, but sweet and exuberant. My daughter wore it for much of her first year, as did my son, eight years later, when he was an infant. Since then, I've knit many sweaters for my children, myself, my husband. I've knit sweaters for my sister, my father, my mother. For the children of friends and in-laws. I have knit many scarves and a few hats (although I still find them annoying). I even knit a toy pig, once, in handspun yarn, with a tail that twirled and black mother-of-pearl buttons for eyes. But I have only knit one sock.

Kroeber's rhythm

On Friday nights, dinner is usually pizza, sometimes Chinese take-out. Or Indian. Beer for my husband and me. Soda for the

kids. Ice cream for dessert. Then we set up in the living room—
pillows, blankets, popcorn—and watch a movie, or, more often,
old TV shows. Generally, we settle on one series at a time,
watching from first episode to last. We saw all three seasons of
Robin Hood in this way, also *The Andy Griffith Show* (until it
went color), *The Flash*, *Seinfeld*, *Poirot*, and *The Green Arrow*.
Currently, we are working our way through *Sherlock*. One of
our favorite shows was the BBC adaptation of James' Herriot's
All Creatures Great and Small, mostly because of Siegfried,
who was funny, and the animals, which were captivating, but
also because of the period detail. It was so interesting to see
those glimpses of prewar England. I remember one scene, for
instance, in which Helen and James are washing dishes after a
church supper; they simply dip each plate into a sink of soapy
water, give it a swirl, and then rub it dry. No running faucet.
No pre-rinse. No post-rinse. Certainly no machine. Another
scene has James searching madly for his second pair of socks,
because that's how many he owns—two—and the first has
gotten muddy while he was birthing a calf.

Nowadays, of course, the majority of people living in
temperate climates own far more than two pairs of socks.
In fact, as previously mentioned, each person on the planet
is said to buy—on average—six new pairs of socks a year
(quite a few more if they happen to be German or Italian[13]).
James Herriot was a veterinarian. He lived a modest but not
an impoverished life. He wore good tweeds and Fair Isle
sweaters. The fact that he owned only two pairs of socks
wasn't presented as a point of drama or real concern, but

merely as an incidental aside—a period detail. It's not too surprising if you stop and consider the fact that, until the mid-twentieth century, a well-made suit was many a man's most expensive personal possession.

In *A History of Hand Knitting*, there is a photograph of a fisherman named John "Sparrow" Hardingham wearing a hand-knit gansey. A gansey is a heavy pullover sweater with textural panels, quite tightly knit so as to keep out the water. The date of this photograph is ca. 1947–1950, but the sweater itself "is thought to have been knitted in the 1920's." In other words, at the time the photograph was taken, the gansey was just about as old as the fisherman wearing it, which is to say around twenty-five. And yet the one is just as fine and fresh as the other (Sparrow was a handsome guy, his sweater pristine).

It's difficult to grasp this idea today, but not too long ago people really did buy and make clothing to last for at least a decade. So clothes were tended, like gardens or homes or animals. They were cared for: ironed, patched, and repaired. Mending was a given. A necessity. But such measures are practically unthinkable today, when to darn a pair of socks or stockings might easily cost more, in terms of time and effort, than to purchase a new pair. That said, there are certainly different ways of calculating costs, and different types of costs, and in some of the most fundamental respects our economy of convenience is exorbitantly expensive.

In 1940, Jane Richardson and Alfred Kroeber published a quantitative analysis of women's fashion in which they established a regular rhythm ("Kroeber's rhythm") for fashion's cycles—a predictable interval of time in which certain qualities of fashion (such as skirt length or neckline depth) could be expected to return or repeat. They calculated this interval to be fifty years. In *The Language of Fashion*, Roland Barthes praises Kroeber's rhythm as being "neither intuitive nor approximate, but precise, mathematical, and statistical." And yet, with typical prescience, he also notes that, "If Kroeber's rhythm were disrupted, it might be due to the growth and globalization of culture, of clothing, of food and by a kind of equalization of cultural objects, of a jostling together that is so intense that the fashion rhythm would be changed. A new history of fashion will begin."[14]

Well, here we are—in that new age, with cycles that spin monthly or faster, so that they're not cycles anymore, but something closer to manic repetitions, a kind of cultural self-soothing. Within this framework, disposability is such a given that only the most practical (and/or the most radically craftivist) among us bother to make or mend our own clothes. What's curious, though—very curious—is how frequently contemporary fashion trends incorporate fake patches, faux-mending jobs, and pretend holes. For example, Gap recently ran an ad campaign involving patches on chinos, with the tagline, "no two are alike." Of course, this was pure fantasy; everything was identical, except for very slight adjustments in the placement of entirely decorative mending jobs. Another example: the other day, walking past Forever 21 on Newbury Street in Boston, I spotted a manikin wearing a T-shirt peppered with tiny holes and a pair of jeans affixed, at knees and thighs, with fake patches only partially covering manufactured tears. But these details are mere winks. Nods. Jokes. Because just as Marie Antoinette didn't want to be a *real* milkmaid, nobody wants *real* holes in their brand new clothes. And yet, there's obviously some kind of appeal in these fake signs of wear. Pretend marks of a pretend past are desirable because they speak to authenticity, even if they are, at the same time, diametrically opposed to it.

It's all about ideas. Brainworlds. Every week, it seems, I find myself newly amazed at the inroads ideas continue to make on material reality, at least when it comes to consumer goods. For example, last Christmas, my sister-in-law gave my daughter an adorable manicure set. It came in a fake leather pouch designed to look like a kitten wearing a Japanese kimono, and inside, the file, nail scissors, and clippers were all painted with red cherry blossoms on a pale yellow ground. The whole set was cute in the extreme. It also looked very well made, sturdy. But not long ago, I had a hangnail and when I tried to trim it with the pretty little scissors, the blades literally bent against my finger. And so the manicure set was not, strictly speaking, an actual manicure set, but merely an idea about what a manicure set might be. Another example: I once bought a wooden rocking chair from Amazon, made, I think, in Georgia. It appeared to be perfectly proportioned and expertly painted—it was slim, elegant, glossy, and black, according to the photograph on Amazon, as well as on the box it came in. But the chair arrived in pieces, heavy pieces, and when my husband finally put them together, the result looked a lot less like a well-made rocking chair with clean, slightly modernist lines, than some kind of bulky torture device built by a handy, if slightly unfocused, fifth grader. Sitting in this chair was a nerve-wracking experience because the center of gravity was set too far back on the rockers— you'd crack your head if you weren't careful. It wasn't my husband's assembly skills at issue (he's an architect); it was just the difference, again, between the idea of a rocking chair and the reality of one. I'd paid for the idea, and it was the idea I got, and, eventually, threw away.

Like this chair, like those nail scissors, like a hundred things I could list (quickly) that have passed through my hands, my home, and my life over the last decade or two, even socks, these days, sometimes achieve a more or less conceptual status. For instance: the violet-colored pair made of 100 percent cashmere (the softest and least durable of all yarns) that I unwisely bought on a mini-spending spree for $26, and that rubbed through at the heel after just three wearings.

Small things

The French have become masters in the art of being happy among "small things," within the space of their own four walls, between chest and bed, table and chair, dog and cat and flowerpot, extending to these things a care and tenderness which, in a world where rapid industrialization constantly kills off the things of yesterday to produce today's objects, may even appear to be the world's last, purely humane corner.

Hannah Arendt, *The Human Condition*

I do other things besides knitting, of course, to try to be a good mother. For example, I once painted our floors with bright green fleur-de-lis, and another time I covered a large branch—a real branch—with tiny paper flowers and brought it inside to hang on the wall. I learned to read children's books out loud with real feeling and I have come a long way, as well, in the art of dispensing, in smallish amounts, not-too-smothering affection. Along with my husband, I have managed to make the kind of home I never knew as a child: a refuge. A place of comfort and love—the easy kind you don't have to think about. I really went all out, not so much with the decorating (there's never been enough cash for that), but with a lot of the "slower" efforts: pies and jams, home grown tomatoes and carrots and chard, soups, breads, a compost heap, and hand-knit sweaters. No socks, sadly, but my kids do have a lot of sweaters. And I think they've had sweet childhoods, so far. But there's only so much you can do as a parent—only so much protection you can provide against larger forces. I might bundle my son up in all seven "veils" on the coldest of days, but he recently turned nine years old and it's become apparent that he understands my maternal protections are merely provisional.

"How long do you think it will take until we're extinct?" he asked me the other day.

"What do you mean?"

"Until it gets so hot we all die. Do you think we'll move to Mars? Or Saturn?"

Plain work

Traditionally, needlework went by two different names, designating two different categories of personal industry, and, by extension, two different social classes. These names were "plain work" and "fancy work," and plain work, as you might imagine, was the less glamorous of the two. It included mending, darning, and the creation of every type of underwear, including socks and stockings. Plain work was necessary work. It took a long time and was poorly paid, and those people engaged in it had little choice. Fancy work, on the other hand, was (at least theoretically) entirely optional. Its purpose, more than anything else, was to exhibit the skills of the needle worker, and the goods produced were generally pretty but unnecessary—things like pineapple bags, ornate pincushions, and lace doilies.

The word "plain" stems from the Latin *planum*, meaning "flat surface," "plane," "level," and "plain," as in a low stretch of land. Plain work, in other words, is mundane work—it is of this world, close to the ground: lowly. Why do we have such disdain for the ground? Why do we associate it with so many negative attributes (the base, the inferior, the pedestrian)? Is it because, as Bataille and Ovid both suggested, our faces (and other key body parts) tilt up? Or is it, perhaps, because we resent gravity itself? The ground's ownership of us? The earth, after all, claims every one of us in the end.

In her preface to *The Human Condition*, Hannah Arendt wrote about the importance the Sputnik launch in 1957 (an "event, second in importance to no other, not even to the splitting of the atom") in regard to our conception of humanity's place in the universe. It was with the Russian satellite, she said, that we realized we are not necessarily bound to the earth, that we might one day leave it behind. Indeed, every indication of our present industrial activity points to this belief. The earth seems more and more like temporary digs, a thing to use up and toss. Just one more consumable demolished by a species that has no patience for plain work.

—

"Ordinary life does not interest me," wrote Anaïs Nin. "I seek only the high moments."

> I want to be a writer who reminds others that these moments exist; I want to prove that there is infinite space, infinite meaning, infinite dimension. But I am not always in what I call a state of grace. I have days of illuminations and fevers. I have days when the music in my head stops. Then I mend socks, prune trees, can fruits, polish furniture. But while I am doing this I feel I am not living.[15]

I get where she's coming from. It seems to me that only a saint could feel exalted while darning socks. But I think it's a good goal. I actually know of just one person who darns his socks on a regular basis and, as a matter of fact, he does seem pretty exalted. I'm talking about a Swedish man named Otto Von Busch, a professor of integrated design at the New School in New York City. Von Busch not only darns his own socks, he also makes his own clothes using secondhand and Goodwill finds that he cuts up, then re-constructs in radical ways. The resulting garments are both silly and somehow fantastic, futuristic. For instance, when I met Von Busch for coffee in New York last winter to discuss his ideas on fashion-based hacktivism (a cousin of craftivism), he wore black pants, black combat boots, an oversized black ribbed sweater, and a voluminous black cape, and every element of this outfit was inexplicably geometric, creating an overall impression of an enormous bat. Although I jotted down what I could from our conversation that morning, my notes are a mess (Von Busch speaks quickly; I write slowly). I do remember this, though—I remember him saying that the opposite of fashion isn't anti-fashion; it's freedom. I also remember that he told me he teaches all of his undergraduates how to darn their own socks. "It's easy!" he shouted. I found him so admirable.

Trimurti

There is in Hindu mythology something called the Trimurti, a trinity composed of the three most important Hindu gods: Brahma (the god of creation), Shiva (the god of destruction), and Vishnu (the god of preservation). Just as their cosmic functions seem to be separate, so the three gods seem to be distinct from one another, and yet the Trimurti suggests inseparability, because ultimately the three forces work together as one ever-shifting, self-adjusting energetic field that keeps the universe in balance.

I think often of the Trimurti when I'm knitting or baking or gardening because when I do these things, I tend to make a mess (à la Shiva), and this annoys my husband. I try to stay tidy, but, to be honest, part of me revels in making messes. Big messes. Sprawling ones. Of course, this isn't fair to the people I live with. I know that. It's just that I get involved. Lose track. Get caught up in the Brahma-spirit of creativity. But what my husband reminds me, again and again, is that when we make one thing, we destroy another. For instance, when I make a sweater, I destroy the living room. And when I make a pie, I destroy the kitchen. But cleaning—tidying up, staying neat—is neither making nor destroying. It is simply an act of preservation. Of conservation. Continuation. Like mending or darning, it's a way of tending. We don't "make" a house, we "keep" it. And all of these acts belong to the realm of Vishnu.

—

A well-known photograph taken on May 2, 1945, shows a man who appears to be Adolf Hitler lying in a pile of rubble in the Chancellery garden in Berlin. Shot in the head, the corpse was discovered by a group of men from the Soviet Counter-Intelligence Unit known as SMERSH. The dead man's toothbrush mustache, the diagonal sweep of his dark hair, and his thin, unsmiling lips all led the Soviets to believe, at first, that they'd found the body of Adolf Hitler. Then someone took a good look at the man's socks, and the group moved on.

Imagine them—the Soviets—bent over the feet of Hitler's body double, surrounded by the waste of war, destruction as far as the eye could see, and then for thousands of miles beyond that. But in that sea of Shiva-spewed carnage, the SMERSH men spotted the one Vishnu-saturated detail that proved beyond the shadow of a doubt that the man with a bullet through his head was too human to be the man they sought: his socks had been darned.

POSTSCRIPT: INSTRUCTIONS FOR DARNING A SOCK

There are a few ways to darn a sock. This is the easiest.

Materials:

- Yarn
- Tapestry needle
- Scissors
- Darning egg or reasonable substitute (e.g., an old-fashioned light bulb or a tennis ball)

Instructions:

1 Turn the sock inside out and center the hole in question over the darning egg (or substitute).

2 Thread the needle with the yarn and make a horizontal line of stitches well beneath the hole, in fabric that is not thinning or unraveling—not even a

little—so as to securely anchor your work. Be sure to make the width of this first line of stitches a bit wider than the hole itself for this same reason (so that as you travel upward, your work will extend beyond any fragile bits of fabric that have developed around the sides of the hole).

3   After you've completed your first row of stitches, turn back and create a second row, slightly above it. As you do so, think like a bricklayer. Try to get some syncopation going: each new stitch should fall roughly above the space between the two stitches below it.

4   Repeat this process until you reach the hole, at which point, don't panic, but simply stretch the working yarn across it. On the other side of the hole, try to pick up the syncopation thing again.

5   Repeat the stranding action every time you traverse the hole, and soon you'll find you've made a miniature ladder.

6   Just as you secured your work in solid fabric at the base of the hole, do so again at the top with a few rows of horizontal stitches.

7   Repeat steps 2 through 6, but now going in the vertical direction. As you proceed, weave every new vertical (warp) strand alternately under or over every horizontal (weft) strand. This will feel fussy and

annoying when you are working with the stitches around the periphery of the hole, but it will be easy and sort of fun when you are dealing with the stranded bits.

8 Weave in the ends and snip the tails flush with the fabric.

9 Teach your friends this simple and economical task. Also any children you may know.

NOTES

Chapter 1

1 Desmond Morris, *The Naked Ape* (New York: Random House, 1967), 42–49.

2 Melissa A. Toups, Andrew Kitchen, Jessica E. Light, et al., "Origin of Clothing Lice Indicates Early Clothing Use by Anatomically Modern Humans in Africa," *Molecular Biology and Evolution* 28, no. 1 (2011): 29–32.

3 History.com staff, "Ice Age," *History.com*, 2015, http://www.history.com/topics/ice-age.

4 Scott Norris, "Humans Wore Shoes 40,000, Fossils Indicate," *National Geographic News* (July 1, 2008), http://news.nationalgeographic.com/news/2008/07/080630-oldest-shoes.html.

5 University College Cork. "World's oldest leather shoe found in Armenia," *ScienceDaily* (June 10, 2010), www.sciencedaily.com/releases/2010/06/100609201426.htm.

6 Marco Iosa, Augusto Fusco, Fabio Marchetti, et al., "The Golden Ratio of Gait Harmony: Repetitive Proportions of Repetitive Gait Phases," *BioMed Research International*, vol. 2013, Article ID 918642, 7 pages, 2013. doi:10.1155/2013/918642.

7   Peter Tyson, "Our Improbable Ability to Walk," *Nova ScienceNOW* (September 20, 2012), http://www.pbs.org/wgbh/nova/body/our-ability-to-walk.html.

8   Ibid.

9   M. David Tremaine and Elias M. Awad, *The Foot & Ankle Sourcebook* (Great Britain: Lowell House, 1998), 11.

10 Joseph A. Amato, *On Foot* (New York: New York University Press, 2004), 5.

11 William A. Rossi, *The Sex Life of Foot and Shoe* (New York: Dutton & Co., 1976), 65.

12 Tremaine and Awad, *The Foot & Ankle Sourcebook*, 50.

13 Hesiod, "*Works and Days*," verse 542.

14 The College of Podiatry, "Feet Facts," http://www.scpod.org/contact-us/press/press-releases/feet-facts/.

15 Brenda Fowler, "Find Suggests Weaving Preceded Settled Life," Science Section, *New York Times* (May 9, 1995).

16 *Harper's Dictionary of Classical Literature*.

17 Roland Barthes, *The Language of Fashion* (Oxford: Berg, 2005), 94.

18 Milton N. Grass, *History of Hoisery* (New York: Fairchild Publications, 1956), 95.

19 Ibid., 116.

20 Jeremy Farrell, *Socks and Stockings* (London: B T Batsford Ltd, 1992), 9.

21 Grass, *History of Hoisery*, 121.

22 Farrell, *Socks and Stockings*, 10.

23 Grass, *History of Hoisery*, 127.

24 Farrell, *Socks and Stockings*, 19.

25 Grass, *History of Hoisery*, 149.

26 Kenrick Vezina, "Socks Generate Electricity Using Socks Fed by Microbes," MIT Technology Review (December 14, 2015), https://www.technologyreview.com/s/544511/socks-generate-electricity-using-microbes-fed-by-urine/.

27 Danielle Braff, "Socks Can Massage, Moisturize, and Cool Your Feet," Lifestyle Section, *Chicago Tribune* (March 16, 2016).

28 Xie Fang, "Datang Socks It to the Financial Crisis," China Daily (April 3, 2009), http://www.chinadaily.com.cn/cndy/2009-03/04/content_7532625.htm.

29 Tania Branigan, "Sock City's Decline May Reveal an Unravelling in China's Economy," The Guardian (September 8, 2012), https://www.theguardian.com/business/2012/sep/09/sock-city-decline-china-economy.

30 "Talking Points and Facts," Population Institute website, https://www.populationinstitute.org/programs/gpso/gpso/.

31 Ibid.

Chapter 2

1 William A. Rossi, "Footwear: the Primary Cause of Foot Disorders," *Podiatry Management* (February 2001), 128–39, http://nwfootankle.com/files/Rossi-FootwearTheprimarycauseofFootDisorders.pdf.

2 C. Scorolli, S. Ghirlanda, M. Enquist, et al., "Relative Prevalence of Different Fetishes," *International Journal of Impotence Research: The Journal of Sexual Medicine* 19 (2007): 423–37.

3   Joseph A. Amato, *On Foot* (New York: New York University Press, 2004), 281.

4   Georges Bataille, *Visions of Excess: Selected Writings, 1927–1939* (Minneapolis: University of Minnesota Press, 1985), 83.

5   G. Stanley Hall, "Some Aspects of the Early Sense of Self," *The American Journal of Psychology* 9, no. 3 (April 1898): 351–95.

6   Paul Hampel, "Belleville Man with Chronic Sock Fetish Charged with Burglary," *St. Louis Post Dispatch* (May 21, 2015).

7   Jim Suhr, "4th Prison Term Looms for Serial Sock-Snatcher," USA Today (July 10, 2008), http://usatoday30.usatoday.com/news/nation/2008-07-10-1043537725_x.htm.

8   John Siddle, "Southport Perverts Who Swindeled Thousands of Socks from Drinkers to Support Bizarre Foot Fetish Inspire New Film," *Echo News* (May 13, 2015), http://www.liverpoolecho.co.uk/news/southport-perverts-who-swindled-thousands-9250839.

9   Stephen G. Michaud and Hugh Aynesworth, *Ted Bundy: Conversations with a Killer* (Irving, TX: Authorlink Press, 2000), 36–37.

10   Tim Marlow, *Schiele* (London: Magna Books, 1990), 17.

11   Rossi, *The Sex Life of Foot and Shoe*, 4.

12   Morris, *The Naked Ape*, 72–73.

13   Michelle Roberts, "Scan Spots Women Faking Orgasms," *BBC News* (June 20, 2005), http://news.bbc.co.uk/2/hi/health/4111360.stm.

14   Janet Lyon, "The Modern Foot," in *Footnotes: on Shoes*, eds. Shari Benstock and Suzanne Ferris (New Brunswick, NJ: Rutgers University Press, 2001), 273.

15 Gaétan Chevalier, Steven T. Sinatra, et al., "Earthing: Health Implications of Reconnecting the Human Body to the Earth's Surface Electrons," *Journal of Environmental and Public Health* 2012 (2012): 291541. PMC. Web. January 26, 2017.

16 Bataille, *Visions of Excess: Selected Writings, 1927–1939*, 260.

Chapter 3

1 J. C. Flügel, *The Psychology of Clothes* (London: Institute of Psycho -Analysis and Hogarth Press. 1930), 83.

2 Bernard Rudofsky, *Are Clothes Modern* (Chicago: Paul Theobald, 1947), 125.

3 Glynis Sweeny, "The Second Dirtiest Thing in the World and You're Wearing It," Altnet.com (August 13, 2015), http://www.alternet.org/environment/its-second-dirtiest-thing-world-and-youre-wearing-it.

4 Michael Shank and Maxine Bédat, "Analysis: Fast Fashion Comes at a Steep Price for the Environment," MSNBC (May 21, 2016), http://www.msnbc.com/msnbc/analysis-fast-fashion-comes-steep-price-the-environment.

5 Zhai Yun Tan, "What Happens When Fashion Becomes Fast, Disposable, and Cheap," NPR (April 10, 2016), http://www.npr.org/2016/04/08/473513620/what-happens-when-fashion-becomes-fast-disposable-and-cheap.

6 As cited in *The True Cost*, the 2015 documentary film directed by Andrew Morgan.

7 Wendy Becktold, "Q&A with Kate Black, America's Ethical Fashion Expert," Sierra Club (November 9, 2015), http://www.

sierraclub.org/sierra/2015-6-november-december/green-life/
qa-kate-black-americas-ethical-fashion-expert.

8   Steve Hargraeves, "Your Clothes Are Killing Us," CNN Money
    (May 22, 2015), http://money.cnn.com/2015/05/22/news/
    economy/true-cost-clothing/.

9   Barthes, *The Language of Fashion*, 116.

10 Ibid., 106.

11 Jessica Pease, "Socks Ed.," pattern download, Ravelry.com
    (2015).

12 Faith Gillespie, "The Masterless Way: Weaving an Active
    Resistance," in *Women and Craft*, ed. Gillian Elinor (London:
    Virago, 1987), 178, as quoted in *Abstract Hactivism the Making
    of a Hacker Culture* by Otto Von Busch and Karl Palmås,
    (London and Istanbul: copyleft by the authors 2006).

13 "The Truth About Europeans' Socks: Europe's Most Extensive
    Survey on Sock Wearing," Blacksocks.com., https://www.
    blacksocks.com/us/en/surveyonsockwearing.

14 Barthes, *The Language of Fashion*, 95.

15 Anaïs Nin, *The Diary of Anaïs Nin*, Vol. 1: 1931–1934
    (New York: Harcourt, 1994), 5.

INDEX

Page references for illustrations appear in *italics*.